Knowledge Management Techniques for Risk Management in IT Projects:

Emerging Research and Opportunities

Muhammad Noman Riaz
National University of Sciences and Technology, Pakistan

A volume in the Advances in IT
Personnel and Project Management
(AITPPM) Book Series

Published in the United States of America by
    IGI Global
    Information Science Reference (an imprint of IGI Global)
    701 E. Chocolate Avenue
    Hershey PA, USA 17033
    Tel: 717-533-8845
    Fax: 717-533-8661
    E-mail: cust@igi-global.com
    Web site: http://www.igi-global.com

Library of Congress Cataloging-in-Publication Data

Names: Riaz, Muhammad Noman, 1982- author.
Title: Knowledge management techniques for risk management in IT projects :
  emerging research and opportunities / by Muhammad Noman Riaz.
Description: Hershey, PA : Information Science Reference, an imprint of IGI
  Global, [2019] | Includes bibliographical references.
Identifiers: LCCN 2018053029| ISBN 9781522583899 (hardcover) | ISBN
  9781522583905 (ebook)
Subjects: LCSH: Information technology projects--Management. | Knowledge
  management. | Risk management. | Project management.
Classification: LCC T58.64 .R53 2019 | DDC 004.068/4--dc23 LC record available at https://lccn.
loc.gov/2018053029

This book is published in the IGI Global book series Advances in IT Personnel and Project Management (AITPPM) (ISSN: 2331-768X; eISSN: 2331-7698)

British Cataloguing in Publication Data
A Cataloguing in Publication record for this book is available from the British Library.

All work contributed to this book is new, previously-unpublished material.
The views expressed in this book are those of the authors, but not necessarily of the publisher.

For electronic access to this publication, please contact: eresources@igi-global.com.

Advances in IT Personnel and Project Management (AITPPM) Book Series

ISSN:2331-768X
EISSN:2331-7698

Editor-in-Chief: Sanjay Misra, Covenant University, OTA, Nigeria & Ricardo Colomo-Palacios, Østfold University College, Norway

MISSION

Technology has become an integral part of organizations in every sector, contributing to the way in which large enterprises, small businesses, government agencies, and non-profit organizations operate. In the midst of this revolution, it is essential that these organizations have a thorough knowledge of how to implement and manage IT projects as well as an understanding of how to attract and supervise the employees associated with these projects.

The **Advances in IT Personnel and Project Management (AITPPM)** book series aims to provide current research on all facets of IT Project Management including factors to consider when managing and working with IT personnel. Books within the AITPPM book series will provide managers, IT professionals, business leaders, and upper-level students with the latest trends, applications, methodologies, and literature available in this field.

COVERAGE

- Project Management Software
- IT Strategy
- IT Personnel Management
- Agile Project Management
- IT Entrepreneurship
- Project Sponsorship
- Outsourcing of IT Projects
- Project Planning
- Communication between Managers and IT Personnel
- Measuring Project Success

IGI Global is currently accepting manuscripts for publication within this series. To submit a proposal for a volume in this series, please contact our Acquisition Editors at Acquisitions@igi-global.com or visit: http://www.igi-global.com/publish/.

Titles in this Series

For a list of additional titles in this series, please visit:
https://www.igi-global.com/book-series/advances-personnel-project-management/77666

Project Portfolio Management Strategies for Effective Organizational Operations
Luca Romano (PMI Central Italy Chapter - CUOA Business School,Italy)
Business Science Reference • ©2017 • 388pp • H/C (ISBN: 9781522521518) • US $200.00

Handbook of Research on Leveraging Risk and Uncertainties for Effective Project Management
Yuri Raydugin (Risk Services & Solutions Inc., anada)
Business Science Reference • ©2017 • 504pp • H/C (ISBN: 9781522517900) • US $275.00

Managing Project Risks for Competitive Advantage in Changing Business Environments
Constanta-Nicoleta Bodea (Bucharest University of Economic Studies, Centre for Industrial and Services Economics, Romania) Augustin Purnus (Technical University of Civil Engineering Bucharest, Romania) Martina Huemann (WU-Vienna University of Economics & Business, Austria) and Miklós Hajdu (Budapest University of Technology and Economics, Hungary)
Business Science Reference • ©2016 • 348pp • H/C (ISBN: 9781522503354) • US $210.00

Strategic Integration of Social Media into Project Management Practice
Gilbert Silvius (LOI University of Applied Sciences, The Netherlands & University of Johannesburg, South Africa)
Business Science Reference • ©2016 • 343pp • H/C (ISBN: 9781466698673) • US $210.00

Strategic Management and Leadership for Systems Development in Virtual Spaces
Christian Graham (University of Maine, USA)
Business Science Reference • ©2016 • 389pp • H/C (ISBN: 9781466696884) • US $210.00

Modern Techniques for Successful IT Project Management
Shang Gao (Zhongnan University of Economics and Law, China) and Lazar Rusu (Stockholm University, Sweden)
Business Science Reference • ©2015 • 374pp • H/C (ISBN: 9781466674738) • US $225.00

For an entire list of titles in this series, please visit:
https://www.igi-global.com/book-series/advances-personnel-project-management/77666

701 East Chocolate Avenue, Hershey, PA 17033, USA
Tel: 717-533-8845 x100 • Fax: 717-533-8661
E-Mail: cust@igi-global.com • www.igi-global.com

Dedicated to my parents and family

Table of Contents

Preface

The primary objective of this study is to examine the tools and techniques of Knowledge Management (KM) and integrate them with Risk Management (RM) techniques for better analysis of risks that occur in different stages of IT projects. The research methodology adopted for the research work is based primary research which encompasses 160 interviews with highly qualified and experienced IT professionals working in public as well as corporate sector organizations of Pakistan. Firstly, the comprehensive and in-depth literature review was conducted related to KM and RM which was followed by the review of the publications of renowned and active national and international organizations that include Ministry of Statistics Govt. of Pakistan, United Nations (UN), World Health Organization (WHO), International Labor Organization (ILO) and many others for the purpose of creating a questionnaire for interview sessions.

For justifying the established framework, the primary research in the form of interview sessions with IT professionals of different and diverse industries (public and corporate sector) of Pakistan were carried out. During the research ten different sources of risks associated with the IT projects were identified that have the potential to threat the success of IT project at any stage of its development life cycle. After that the relevant tools and techniques of KM were implemented to analyze the risks followed by scrutnization of the similarities existing between KM and RM.

As far as the practical implications of this study is concerned the findings as well as the recommendation to the best of authors knowledge are applicable to all the project based organizations that are practicing or intend to practice the tools and techniques of KM for the purpose of RM. Besides, the industrial sector the findings as well as the recommendations being proposed by the study also help the academia to come up with the novel framework / solution of the integration of KM and RM tools and techniques either independently or in close collaboration with the industrial sector.

To the best of the author's knowledge this is the first attempt to find out the commonalities between two distinct domains of Project Management (PM) i.e. KM and RM, and in what manner they can be integrated together and paves the way for more advance future studies.

Muhammad Noman Riaz
National University of Sciences and Technology, Pakistan
Islamabad, Pakistan, 23 Jan. 2019

Acknowledgment

I offer my profound regard and blessing to everyone who supported me in any respect during the completion of my thesis. Also not forgetting my parents, my mentors, they in every way offered much assistance before, during and at completion stage of this studywork. I deeply appreciate their support. Thank you so much.

Muhammad Noman Riaz
National University of Sciences and Technology, Pakistan

Introduction

BACKGROUND OF STUDY

PM established as a distinct area of the organization from engineering domain in the later part of the decade of 1990s. The emphasis of the process of PM was laid on planning and on a planning of a certain project and regulating budgets (Boddy *et al.*, 2009). Due to the amplified complications and the fiasco of the process to contain the individuals operating on the project, this model commenced to flop in the initial part of 2000 decade (Boddy *et al.*, 2009). It is mentioned in a report that claims that the PM theory has been outdated, (Koskela *et al.*, 2002) claimed that PM utilized the "planning-execution-controlling" processes of handling a project, and both of them have altered these processes to "planning", "task dispatching" for the implementation of the project, and a "thermostat model" for regulating the project. As per this model, all PM involves the planning of project, assignment of tasks, and after that performs the project monitoring to ensure that the project is running as per the given schedule. This perception has been changed and there is a further emphasis on the management of knowledge in project. For instance, *"A Guide to the Project Management Body of Knowledge (PMBOK®)"* includes ten knowledge areas of (i) "integration management",(ii) "scope management", (iii) "time management", (iv) "cost management", (v) "quality management", (vi) "human resources management", (vii) "communications management", (viii) "risk management", (ix) "procurement management", and (x) "stakeholder management" (PMI, 2013).

The latest Information Technology projects are accomplished or managed by applying the PM model as defined in the *"PMBOK®"*. That particular model ensures the management of the scope of the project, cost of the project, and time objectives in order to deliver the project which meets or exceeds the needs of both the end user and all the stakeholders (Schwalbe *et al.*., 2010). The PM deals all types of issues ranging from the technology, organization and business standpoints whereas managing the objectives of the project as well as put scope, time and costs in equilibrium (Schwalbe *et al..*, 2010). The model of PM utilizes the Information Technology "project life cycle" which starts with a conceptual phase, then comes the development phase, then implementation phase, and in the end a closing phase (Schwalbe *et al.*, 2010).. It is considered that the process of the PM is simple for employees or professionals of the organization to pursue, as revealed by the authors of (Chou *et al.*, 2013) in their research work titled, the "Use of the PM process in construction industry in Taiwan, Indonesia, and Vietnam".KM is basically related to the management of knowledge in the organization. KM is established as organizations those have learnt the worth and significance of knowledge and the manner by which they could practice it to gain a competitive advantage (Tiwana *et al.*, 2002). As the research of the authors of (Davenport *et al.*, 1998) revels, the knowledge is primarily a blend of values, experiences, insights gain from the experts' eyes and contextual information which provides a foundation for assessing fresh information and experiences . Information is termed as the foundation for any type of knowledge. The authors in (Nonaka *et al.*, 1995) termed information as "the flow of messages with meaning to the individual and knowledge is created by the flow of information". The authors have measured knowledge to be "actionable information". Information is generated from the available data that are a set of neutral facts related to a particular event. In the process of generating knowledge, the authors (Boisot *et al.*, 1998) have deliberated the formation of a set of potentials for the event. Centered upon these prospects, a person is to initiate the actions. The KM tools as recognized by the authors (Wang *et al.*, 2011), which contain "mind maps", "concept maps", "conceptual diagrams", and "visual metaphors" which are being utilized in KM.

The tools of both KM and PM are utilized to share and organize the knowledge relevant to the project. Table 1 classifies few KM and PM tools. Dissimilar tools are utilized to share knowledge with diverse stakeholders. The authors have separated the tools into different knowledge areas as mentioned in the "*PMBOK*"®. The knowledge areas mentioned in the *PMBOK*® are (i) "integration management", that synchronizes the processes of a project, (ii) "scope management"—what is included and what is not included in the project, (iii) "time management", (iv) "cost management", (v) "quality management", (vi) "human resources management", (vii) "communications management", (viii) "risk management", (ix) "procurement management" encompasses the procurement of assets, and (x) "stakeholder management" requires for the processes which encompass all the stakeholders and stakeholders' expectations.

Table 1. Comparison of the uses of PM tools and KM tools

Project Management Tool	Use	KM Tool	Use
Gantt Chart	Time Management	Mind Map	Organization
Work Break Down Structure	Time Management	Concept Map	Organization
Flow Chart	Integration Management	Data Repositories	Acquiring Information
Cost/Benefit Analysis	Cost Management	Discussion Boards	Communication

INTRODUCTION

The purpose of the author's research work was to discover the gap among the uses of Knowledge Management, (KM), Risk Management (RM) and Project Management (PM) tools and techniques in Information Technology (IT) projects. The organizations have been involved in consuming projects in the fields of construction, engineering, IT and defense, and IT to fetch out strategic change and generate competitive advantage for the previous 50 years or so. The modern-day organizations have been producing large number of projects than in the preceding years due to continuously varying market situations, technological developments, and legal formalities. As a consequence, the fiasco rate of IT projects has turn out to be extraordinary. In the year 1994, the "Standish Group" published its *"Chaos Report"*, which showed that almost 31% of IT related projects in that very year were disastrous; approximately 16% of those finished productively, whereas the rest 53% were reflected as "challenged". Such figures have enhanced since 1994. In the year 2009, 24% of projects were unsuccessful while 32% were measured as successful; but, there still exists the reason of concern (Eveleens *et al.*, 2010).

Even though PM is utilized in construction, engineering, and the development of businesses, this study emphasis on IT projects and the use of KM techniques for risk management in the process. In today's world IT PM refers to the use of knowledge, tools, and techniques for a specified project to be supplied centered on the necessities of the project. For the most of the parts, organizations exercise PM practices to consolidate and plan the work of IT projects. Hence, a substantial quantity of knowledge essentially be managed amongst the dissimilar stakeholders in the project. The huge quantity of knowledge be able to be managed in an IT project proposes that it could be conceived by the members of project team as a part of knowledge process in organizations.

The author has scrutinized the role of KM tools and techniques for risk management in IT projects. By thoughtful course of knowledge in IT project, the model for IT PM can be upgraded and IT projects can be more fruitful than in the preceding times. The purpose of this research work was to address the key issue of in what way to practice KM tools and techniques ca be used to aid increase the performance of IT projects.

Problem Statement

The aim of the research study is as follows:

To discover the degree to which KM tools and techniques are appropriate to the procedures and processes of RM utilized in different stages of Information Technology based projects. This additionally examines whether they can be successfully applied in order to develop existing RM practices.

Objectives of the Study

For the recognition of the aim, the objectives for research work were defined. They are stated below:

1. To identify risks associated with IT projects.
2. To scrutinize and validate KM Tools and Techniques and explore its commonalities with RM techniques for effective risk analysis in IT projects.

Scope and Delimitations

The research work provides evidence regarding IT projects in different organizations of Pakistan, discussing how KM is applied in the projects, and conceivable developments that KM provides in this setting. Even though the facts and figures obtained after this research is prized to other organizations, the suggestions after this research may not be freely exchangeable to the entire range of contexts where Project Knowledge Management (PKM) initiatives are being deliberated or have been employed. Supplementary research work may be necessary to practice the outcomes in Pakistan and the exchange of knowledge in this process was studied in the research. The transfer of knowledge outside of Pakistan may not be similar, and PKM may require suitable processes and techniques outside of Pakistan.

This research work receives the concern of project fiasco because of unsuitable risk management into consideration to discover the risks that threat the project from the establishment stage. This can be achieved by seeing this framework from the lens of KM. This can be stuck due to the fact that numerous projects experience fiasco as a consequence of the lack of knowledge amongst the project stakeholders or dearth of information sharing as the project in hand advances.

One of the innovative and noteworthy areas of research which has not been discovered comprehensively before is KM process employment for the assistance for the purpose of RM processes application. That shapes the theme of this research work. The conventional PM approaches focus of sources of risk that are regular in nature, the outcome of project cannot be reasonably anticipated if the potential areas of risks associated to the use of information are not recognized and analyzed. By means of formation and dissemination of knowledge, the worth of organization as well as its competency is improved to reply to novel and uncommon circumstances that could otherwise guide to risk formation. Furthermore, the use of a knowledge-based approach possesses the capacity for filtering the services and abilities of risk managers.

This research work undertakes the above elaborated issues keeping in view the context of the project in different stages of the project when the scope of the project and expectations of the stakeholders are made clear. It can be realized at this particular stage that an information can be lost if it is not managed properly. Thus the scope of the study was defined with a comprehensive analysis of risks and their management by means of the use of KM resources in shape of tools, skills, approaches and techniques.

Research Questions

The following questions have been examined in this research work:

RQ1: In what way a KM be used in PM for IT projects?
RQ2: In what way are the tools and techniques for KM used in IT PM to increase the success rate of an IT project?
RQ3: In what way the existing PM process handling knowledge for an IT project?

RQ4: In what way does the PKM model for handling knowledge improve the success of an IT project?

RQ5: To what extent, in your esteemed organization, the KM practices are developed or mature?

RQ6: In what manner would you describe the application or utilization of KM in your esteemed organization?

RQ7: Do your organization has any documented policy as far KM tools & techniques are concerned?

RQ8: At what extent your organization practices the tools, techniques or methods (Storytelling, Benchmarking, Brainstorming etc.) for KM?

RQ9: At what extent your organization practices the tools, techniques or methods (SWOT, PESTEL, FMEA etc.) for RM?

RQ10: To what extent the sources of risk (like information unavailability, inappropriate flow of information etc.) affects your esteemed organization?

RQ11: In your viewpoint how the techniques and approaches of KM & RM share similarities?

RQ12: In your perspective, is there any scope available for incorporating KM tool & techniques into RM tool & techniques?

RQ13: Would you like to give any suggestions / recommendations for KM and RM as well as for joint functioning?

Significance of Study

Project accomplishment is made clear as when the project is finished and executes the desires of the end user. The project is finished inside time limits and budget supplies and the entire chain of stakeholders feel content. The author of present literature deliberated in what way KM would improve PM in IT, however they failed to highlight by what means it was applied in the organization. This study considered the gap in literature by reviewing in what way KM is being utilized in PM in IT for an insurance company. I examined KM in the different phases of an IT project and the impact on the success of the project. The research focused on defining whether_or_not_the KM tools and techniques can aid the project to become a success.

Significance to Practice

IT projects are mainly engineered by software engineers or programming experts who are respected due to their skill to create computer or software systems. They usually cannot be rewarded for sharing knowledge in IT projects.

Sharing of knowledge is important for the accomplishment of the project, which proposes that a revolution is desirable in the manner software developers are rewarded. The PKM model recognizes where knowledge essentially be handled and organized in the PM process. It recognizes the crucial facets of the process in which knowledge sharing is desired for an effective project.

Significance to Theory

The current research work is focused on the improvement of PM processes by integrating the tools and techniques of KM and RM. This effort will likely to improve the process of knowledge sharing among all the stakeholders of the project and members of the project team, in this way the understanding about the project can be realized at its optimum. In this way as the authors (Adolph *et al.*, 2011) said that the knowledge sharing resolves different perspectives exist. The authors like (Hanish *et al.*, 2011) recommended that in a project, the key activity is a learning of the team members, who learn from the knowledge of the project to make a project successful. As the authors (Karpicke *et al.*, 2012) have pointed out retrieval of the information is critical to learning. The tools and repositories an organization use for KM must have appropriate ways to retrieve the information or learning by the project team members will be challenged.

Significance to Social Change

According to the research of the authors (Anantatmula *et al.*, 2008) accomplished IT projects generate openings for the organization. Such openings can guide to better social environments. Organizations can mature a diversity of dissimilar types of IT projects. The accomplishment of some projects is affected by what means the project knowledge is organized and managed. This contains projects for the betterment of society.

This study may adjust the manner in which PM is imparted in the lecture halls of educational institutes. As a university professor, I have been teaching courses associated to KM, RM and PM for the last 2 years. I have witnessed the significance of KM in the PM process and the difficulties which can arise while KM is not chunk of the process. There erupts a necessity for

IT project teams to comprise KM in the project process and this study will make available a model for organizations. The KM concepts must be made a part of PM courses (as to the best of the author's knowledge no university in Pakistan offers a course on KM in Project Management degree) to aid students study knowledge sharing matters and the influence they can have on the project. The students must know in what way to plan and correct the KM disputes in the process of PM.

Organization and Structure of the Study

The structure and organization of the research studyis given below:

In Chapter 1 of the research work, the author tries to cover the literature review KM. The literature review will begin by classifying the basic concepts into its segments which will followed by the process of knowledge conversion. After that the concept of KM is highlighted and subsequently the domains techniques and categorization of KM will be discussed in depth. Also, in the same chapter we have carried out a thorough literature review regarding Risk Management (RM). This has been accomplished by the classification of different types of risks has been presented followed by the differentiation between risk and uncertainty. Finally, the last section describes sources of risks that affects the execution of IT project.

Chapter 2 of this study using the qualitative approach was to discover the gap that exists among the uses of PM, RM and KM tools and techniques used in various IT projects. The primary objective of the current chapter was to propose an appropriate research methodology practiced for assessing and examining KM, RM and PM during the undertaking the IT projects as well as to comprehend by what means KM and RM become a part of PM. This chapter focuses on the framework around which research structure is centered. It can be elaborated in terms of research design and rationale followed by role of the researcher. The next segment of this chapter focusses on the justification of utilizing interviews as a primary data collection tool. After this the explanation of data processing and data analysis methodology was used. The last segment elaborates the issues related to trustworthiness and throws light on ethical procedures.

Chapter 3 makes available the analysis of collected information for the sole reason of research. Firstly, it has been prepared for the conduct of secondary research, that shapes an appropriate way for the purpose of primary research framework, then the information collected by virtue of several conducted interviews was then examined and analyzed. Hence, develops the basis the platform on which the discussion is founded. In the last section of this chapter we presented the trustworthiness evidence of our research work.

Chapter 4 offers a thorough deliberation about the available information in the shape of scrutinized data both collected by means of primary and secondary sources gathered due to in hand research work. To accomplish this deliberation pursues the aims and objectives of the research that are reliant on one another and hence track an order. Firstly, the interpretation of findings have been carried out which will be followed by an in-depth analysis of the first objective of this research study. After that the thorough discussion was made by examining and scrutinizing the last three objectives of this study.

The Conclusion of the research work is divided into sections which encompass the fulfillment of research aim and objectives, elaborate the study by providing the practical implications of the research work, research limitations, future research directions & recommendations for more advance studies in the field of Project Management.

REFERENCES

Aghili, S. (2010). Organizational risk management: Successful achievement of business objectives hinges on the organization's ability to manage risk effectively. *Internal Auditor, 67*(3).

Alhawaria, S., Karadshehb, L., Taletc, A. N., & Mansoura, E. (2011). Knowledge-Based Risk Management framework for Information Technology project. *International Journal of Information Management, 32*(1), 50-65. doi:10.1016/j.ijinfomgt.2011.07.002

Antvik, S., & Sjöholm, H. (2007). *Project: Management and methods.* Västerås: Projektkonsult Håkan Sjöholm AB.

APM. (2006). *A PM Body of Knowledge (5ᵗʰ ed.).* Buckinghamshire, UK: Association for Project Management.

Arrow, J. (2008). *Knowledge-Based Proactive Project Risk Management.* AACE International Transactions.

Artto, K. A., Kähkönen, K., & Pitkänen, P. J. (2000). *Unknown Soldier Revisited: Story of Risk Management* (5th ed.). Helsinki: Project Management Association.

Aven, T. (2010). *Misconceptions of Risk.* Chichester, UK: John Wiley and Sons Ltd.

Baldeon, C., & Arribas-Baños, M. D. (2008). *Management Information Systems in Social Safety Net Programs: A Look at Accountability and Control Mechanisms.* Washington, DC: The World Bank. Available at: http://siteresources.worldbank.org/SOCIALPROTECTION/Resources/SP-Discussion-papers/Safety-Nets-DP/0819.pdf

Bellinger, G., Castro, D., & Mills, A. (2004). *Data, Information, Knowledge, and Wisdom.* Available at: http://www.systems-thinking.org/dikw/dikw.htm

Berg, B. L. (2009). *Qualitative Research Methods for the Social Sciences (7th ed.).* Boston: Pearson Education.

Bernstein, P. L. (1998). *Against the Gods: The Remarkable Story of Risk.* Oxford, UK: John Wiley & Sons.

Binder, J. C. (2007). *Global Project Management: Communication, Collaboration and Management Across Borders.* Hampshire, UK: Gower Publishing Limited.

Boddy, D. (2002). *Managing Projects: Building and Leading the Team.* Essex, UK: Pearson.

Chapter 1
Literature Review

ABSTRACT

In this chapter of the research work, the author tries to cover the literature review of KM and RM. The literature review will begin by classifying the basic concepts into its segments, which will be followed by the process of knowledge conversion. After that the concept of KM is highlighted, the domains techniques and categorization of KM will be discussed in depth. Also, the authors have carried out a thorough literature review regarding risk management (RM). This has been accomplished by the classification of different types of risks followed by the differentiation between risk and uncertainty. Finally, the last section describes sources of risks that affect the execution of IT projects.

DOI: 10.4018/978-1-5225-8389-9.ch001

CLASSIFICATION OF KM

Before we dive in the vast domain of KM, it seems necessary to make clear the distinctive terms of data, knowledge, information and wisdom. The nature of Data is uncooked or raw with no significant meaning elsewhere its presence (Kothar *et al.*, 2004). Information is considered as the processed arrangement of data that conveys some meaning (Bellinger *et al.*, 2004). Knowledge can be defined as the cognizance or comprehension attained by interpretative joining of data by means of experience and information. In short, when data and information considers with certain perception that becomes a knowledge. Wisdom is the eventual terminal and is termed as assessed and polished blend of knowledge and experience. Figure 1 clarifies the transformational relationship between the terms, knowledge and experience.

The authors of Ikujiro Nonaka and Hirotaka Takeuchi subsidized to the domain of knowledge by presenting the categorization and understanding of knowledge. Both the authors have categorized knowledge into two categories that is: "Explicit" and" Tacit" that shapes the foundation of KM in capturing the part contributed by information as well as human systems. "Explicit knowledge" is a type of a knowledge that can be apprehended and deposited in the shape of documents for the purpose of record keeping (Nonaka *et al.*, 1995). It can also be termed as the "hard aspect of knowledge" and is typically autonomous of context. This by virtue of nature is depictive and can be improved or altered according to the usage to augment its variety of value. Its process of transformation will occur by transforming the knowledge

Figure 1. Transition of Intellectect
(Bellinger et al., 2004)

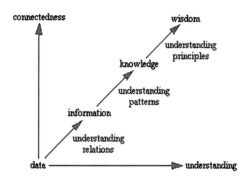

into information and at that time information into data. "Tacit knowledge" by nature exists in the intelligence of beholder and that entity can either be a person l or a group of people (Nonaka *et al.*, 1995). Since it is founded on wisdom and experience, its recording is not possible. It can also be termed as the '"soft aspect of knowledge" and is generally inserted in a certain context.

Knowledge Management Definition

By virtue of the explanation of knowledge available at present, the notion of KM can be grasped. The definition of KM fluctuates from corner to corner of organizations and industries with the emphasis on the employment of knowledge for the purpose of "organizational competitiveness" distant from the non-profit and for-profit organizations. NASA terms it as "the conveyance of precise information to the right people at the accurate time while assisting a single persons in the creation and sharing of knowledge to utilize information to evidently improve performance".

Few authors define KM keeping in view its functionality. KM is all about figuring out *"who gets what when and how"* (Choucri *et al.*, 2007). Some researchers sponsor it by recognizing it as a process instead of a function. The researchers recognize knowledge as a "mental substance", exist in in a single person minds and demonstrated in writings and actions, instead of a process that confines its understanding (Nocolini *et al.*, 2003). The KM process begins from the identification and examination of open and vital information heading to the consequential planning and regulating of actions to breed knowledge resources (Chawla *et al.*, 2010).

As a whole, KM functions as a structural process to elucidate the professional requirements to combine the organizational preferences and objectives to provide maintainable benefits. Even though there exists various interpretations of the concept of KM, there are matches available as far as the purpose and application of KM is concerned.

Knowledge Management Techniques

The main methods, techniques and tools applied to satisfy the above-mentioned domains are elaborated below:

Forming Communities of Practice (COP's)

The "COP" is a virtual community or unceremonious group backed by an organization to assist sharing of knowledge and teach (Cox *et al.*, 2005). They are shaped by the people who take part in developments of mutual learning in a cooperative field of human struggle. In naiver terms, it is regularly a natural shaping of net of personnel with like interests, experience or skills.

H1: There is an impact of COPs in the effective analysis of risks in IT projects

Creation and Utilization of Knowledge Database

The database of knowledge is a category related to repository of knowledge utilized for the purpose of "bookmarking", "searching" and "exploiting" the necessary. That thing in few organizations, is also termed as the "best practices database". Various terminology is linked with it through organizations. The technical terms contain "DMS (Document Management Systems)", "Knowledge banks", "Document repositories" and many others. The database of such an information is valuable in organizations where top practices must be reiterated and distributed as abundantly as possible (Fugate *et al.*, 2009).

H2: There is an impact of Creation & Utilization of Knowledge Database in the effective analysis of risks in IT projects

Incorporation of Lessons Learnt Into Strategies

The process of project is a torrent of fresh learning. The degeneration of knowledge is possible with the addition of like errors being recurrent till the time the experience attained in some project is diffutilized to the strategic level of organizational and practiced in some other projects. As a consequence of this, the learnt lessons must be exploited to add them in the strategic plan causing the development for top practices.

H3: There is an impact of Lessons Learnt in the effective analysis of risks in IT projects

Brainstorming Sessions

Brainstorming is considered as one of the most pursued techniques for the formation or creation of knowledge. The process offers abundant answers to problems by extending ideas to the maximum. Asa consequence it inspires "cross-fertilization" of ideas offering confidence to personnel to accept top practices . It lastly will take to the integration of mutual thinking with common mental models.

H4: Brainstorming Sessions contribute effectively in the analysis of risks in IT projects

Establishing Knowledge Maps

"Knowledge mapping" is a process of generating a web of knowledge repository by localizing and shaping the scholarly assets. It controls the experience and skills by giving a forum for methodical evaluation and approachability of the organizational associates' proficiencies to everybody. Other technical representations for this contain the "Expertise Locator (EL) system", "Hard-Tagging" where this process is to be pursued but with a emphasis on the prescribed mentoring process. The concept is built on the impression that most knowledge generally resides inside the organization and does not require to bring in and hence only requires to be recognized, caught and harnessed.

H5: There is a relationship between Establishing Knowledge Maps in the effective analysis of risks in IT projects

Performing Knowledge Audit

The KM related literature distinguishes the significance of two concepts: the first and foremost is the investigation and analysis of present knowledge practices for the purpose of gap identification and the second and last is to link the business goals with KM. "Information Management (IM)" as a main component of KM answers the first purpose by offering a mean to examine knowledge to achieve organizational goals in the shape of the audit of information. The "information audit" is a methodical examination of information assets, their use and flow, with alignment in the direction of individuals and present documents for establishing associations to organizational goals.

The audit of knowledge analyzes the efficiency of organization in the use of information and the orientation of information assets and processes in the direction of the organizational goals. This is accomplished by classifying the tasks and activities as well as the information needed by them that lead to the achievement of business objectives. Besides this, the audit inspects where, by whom and how the information initiates, and then where it move to, to whom it is given and what occurs to it after that. This flow of information attaches strategic meaning to information thus supporting in handling pertinent information by prioritizing. Fiasco in prioritization by means of strategic implication to organization can take to handling everything as an alternative of precisely what would be achieved.

H6: There is an impact of Performing Knowledge Audit in the effective analysis of risks in IT projects

Benchmarking

Benchmarking is considered as one of the tools for carrying out the procedures of monitoring as well reporting. It has the capability to explain the purpose of producing "explicit knowledge" for the organizations by assessing and reporting the scholarly assets. It offers a framework for the development of the organization by describing a contrast with the industry level standards in the shape of level of competency, the possessed capability and embedded knowledge. Furthermore, benchmarking of inner KM processes creates obvious knowledge gaps across the entire range of stakeholders (Chawla *et al.*, 2010).

H7: There is an impact of Benchmarking in the effective analysis of risks in IT projects

Besides this key aforementioned tools and techniques, the other minimum utilized KM strategies for businesses comprise of the "practice of giving rewards" (sharing of knowledge by means of motivation), "storytelling "(for conveying tacit knowledge)," cross-project learning" by means of transfer of knowledge and people, "reviews" after some action has performed (for the purpose of creation of top Practices), "knowledge fairs" (for the involvement of stakeholder), using "collaborative technologies "(groupware, etc.), through the use of "social software" (wikis, social bookmarking, blogs, etc.). Like these strategies and methods of KM must be realistic in practice for the purpose of presence, their efficacy is reliant on the readiness and energetic contribution of the people as "knowledge workers".

H8: There is an impact of Practice of Giving Rewards in the effective analysis of risks in IT projects

H9: There is an impact of After Action Reviews in the effective analysis of risks in IT projects

H10: There is an impact of Knowledge Fairs in the effective analysis of risks in IT projects

The classification of different types of risks has been presented followed by the differentiation between risk and uncertainty. This chapter then focusses on RM processes and its techniques being used for risk management purposes. After that the RM constraints have been discussed. Finally, the last section describes sources of risks that affects the execution of IT project.

Classification of Risk

The Risks are able to be broadly classified into two types: the ones which are related with the management of in-house assets / resources and hence are controllable while the other type deals with the external assets / resources and comparatively uncontrollable in nature (Carr *et al.*, 2001). This is because of the fact that the relationship of probability associated with the external factors / environment is quite large with randomness while in case of internal resources form the events of risks which would be calculated and determined probability and impact / consequence product. As far as internal capabilities are concerned, the planning of risk can be augmented by utilizing the knowledge and experience gained by several managers while executing and working on numerous projects. The approach to sense and reply to risks, defines how deep the organization possesses the scholarly capital in terms of judgement and knowledge.

Risks Project Outlook

In the framework of project, risk can be considered as a "disorder", the recognition of that clues towards the deviation from the project goals and objectives of cost, quality, scope, time and others (Zhang *et al.*, 2007). By means of the standpoint of available information, risks in their entirety are termed as a clusters of factors developed on the basis of varied stakeholders' perspective. By means of the viewpoint of the in-hand project, risks may ascend by means of the operational / business facets. During the initial stages of project, the more emphasis or stress is given to business risks while during the execution or implementation of the project the operational risks are of primary importance. As it has been researched that the business risks have the potential to adversely affect the particular work activities while the risks associated with the business disturb the entire in—hand project(Dey *et al.*, 2007(.

Risk Management Definition

As different entities and organizations define RM in different expressions and styles, the field and domain of RM has become more complex due to diversity in interpretation. The "International Standard Organization" (ISO) defines it as "a set of coordinated functions or activities applied in order to control and direct the organization with concern to risks"(ISO, 2009). The "Association of Project Management "(APM), on the other hand, defines RM as, "A structured process that allows individual risk events and overall project risk to be understood and managed proactively, optimizing project success by minimizing threats and maximizing opportunities" (APM 2006).

The "Institute of Risk Management" recognizes it as, "The process whereby organization methodically addresses the risks attaching to their activities with the goal of achieving sustained benefit within each activity and across the portfolio of all activities" (IRM 2002).

But no matter which ever definition is utilized, the RM whole purpose always remain identical that is to integrate approaches and information from the diverse parts of a project on a specific facet of uncertainty. Hence, RM is considered essential to put emphasis on the previous difficulties and problems heading to complications, current challenges and main preferences that threaten the fruitful implementation of the project.

Uncertainty and Knowledge

As it is depicted in Figure 2, during the phase of project execution, the risk decreases when the knowledge about the project increases. This depicts that at the beginning of a project, several risks of qualitative nature are available that decrease with the availability and access of information.

In all the phases the projects are bounded by risks and the actions to respond are identified, evaluated and cautiously selected on the source of the knowledge reckonable at that particular stage (Noori *et al.*, 2009). A RM proactive methodology as elaborated by UNESCO supports learning from experience for the purpose of anticipation, recognition and the management of both threats and opportunities inherently presently in risks (UNESCO 2009).

That will be achieved by beginning the RM processes timely in the project lifecycle to exploit the potential of the engagement process of the complete range of project stakeholders in a process. During the initial stages of a project, the risks linked are built on the uncertainty that confines making decisions to lead a project. That element of uncertainty can well be defined as a condition due to which there exists an absence of information. Procedures for undertaking the risks will be instigated if abundantly precise information

Figure 2. Risk and Knowledge Change during the Project
(Noori et al., 2009)

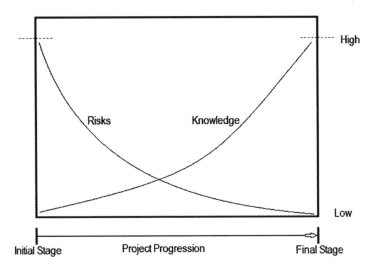

is reachable. This creates the recognition of qualitative risks essential initially in the starting phase of project besides evaluating their probability as well as impact (Isaac *et al.*, 2011)

Concerning the dilemma of an information domain, Duncan (1972) explains on three characteristics hampering the decision making process in vigorous settings:

1. A scarcity lies in accessible information
2. Incapability to measure the consequence of an inappropriate decision in advance
3. Incapability to give probabilities to foresee consequences or outcomes

Goal of Risk Management

The goal of RM is to handle the entire range of the risks inborn in project and in the context of it. It can be implemented by managing risks on the foundation of regularity of occurrence, impact level, significance, after that by desirable arrangement to regulate the recognized risks. Risks can be categorized into two segments built on their structure: risks that costs can be projected that is quantifiable risks and the other risks which financial effects could not be directly predicted that is, qualifiable risks (Franke *et al.*, 1999) that shapes the foundation for the following section.

Sources of Risks in IT Projects

It is a well-known fact that the management of IT project like construction project management cannot be escaped from the risks that are the creation of nearby environmental conditions. In view of the above, it seems mandatory that a thorough understanding of all known risks at a deeper level is required that helps in the formulation of strategic policy to counter the risks in order to make an IT project a success. It is a myth that prevails in many of IT professionals as well IT related organizations that only the financial risks are capable of hampering the execution and completion of IT projects. But on the real side, several researches and surveys have revealed that not only financial constraints affects the execution process of the IT project but also there are several other risks associated with IT projects. So, the IT project managers must have to view this aspect in a holistic manner rather than solely focusing on financial issues. The project managers of IT projects must try to prevent the situation in the beginning of its eruption before it develops into a problem of larger magnitude that eventually will lead to an ultimate and irreparable disaster.

It is also pertinent to mention here that the organizations, whether they are directly related to the development of IT projects or the organizations which have dedicated IT department to undertake their routine tasks face all types of known risks on daily basis due to constantly changing the environment of the world. The internal as well as the external environment of the organization breeds the development of the risks that forcefully hampers the monitoring as well as the risk mitigation techniques. So, if the organizations continue to breed the sources of risks, they will greatly impact the existing as well as the future organization related with IT project in one way or the other.

After the in depth scrutiny of available literature, the IT related projects range from the development of an application software, a software for telecommunication equipment, a software for missile system of sea vessels etc. There are numerous risks attached with IT projects some of them are Risk of Information, Risk associated with Human Resources, Risk of Success, Rapid Changes in Technology, Financial Risks, Risk associated with the Management etc.

Figure 3. Conceptual framework

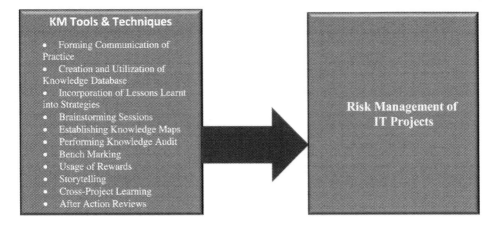

THEORETICAL FRAMEWORK

Based on the study of the literature, with reference to the variables identified in the envisioned study the relationship between the variables have been established as depicted in the theoretical framework / conceptual model in Figure 3. Figure 3 depicts that the implementation of KM Tools and Techniques (independent variables) may mitigate different types of risks associated with IT projects (dependent variable). By virtue of primary research the author will try to proof the under mentioned theoretical model.

REFERENCES

Boddy, D., Boonstra, A., & Kennedy, G. (2009). Managing Information Systems: Strategy and Organisation (3rd ed.). Essex, UK: Pearson Education Limited.

Bolisani, E., & Damiani, F. (2010). Knowledge management in complex environments: The UN peacekeeping. *Measuring Business Excellence, 14*(4), 76-84. doi:10.1108/13683041011093776

Bresnen, M., Goussevskaia, A., & Swan, J. (2004). Embedding New Management Knowledge in Project-Based Organizations. *Organization Studies, 25*(9), 1535-1555. doi:10.1177/0170840604047999

Carr, V., & Tah, J. H. M. (2001). A fuzzy approach to construction project risk assessment and analysis: Construction project risk management system. *Advances in Engineering Software, 32*(10-11), 847-857. doi:10.1016/S0965-9978(01)00036-9

Chapman, C., & Ward, S. (2003). *Project Risk Management (2nd ed.)*. Chichester, UK: John Wiley and Sons Ltd.

Chawla, D., & Joshi, H. (2010). Knowledge management practices in Indian industries–A comparative study. *Journal of Knowledge Management, 14*(5), 708-725. doi:10.1108/13673271011074854

Choi, B., & Lee, H. (2002). *Knowledge management strategy and its link to knowledge creation process. Expert Systems with Applications, 23(3)*, 173–187. doi:10.1016/S0957-4174(02)00038-6

Choi, B., Poon, S. K., & Davis, J. G. (2006). Effects of knowledge management strategy on organizational performance: A complementarity theory-based approach. *Omega: The International Journal of Management Science*, 235-251. doi:10.1016/j.omega.2006.06.007

Choucri, N. (2007). The Politics of Knowledge Management. Massachusetts Institute of Technology. Available at http://www.portal.unesco.org/education/es/files/54909/...pdf/Choucri.pdf

Coakes, E., Amar, A. D., & Granados, M. L. (2010). Knowledge management, strategy, and technology: A global snapshot. *Journal of Enterprise Information Management, 23*(3), 282-304. doi:10.1108/17410391011036076

Chapter 2
Research Methodology

ABSTRACT

The purpose of this study using the qualitative approach was to discover the gap that exists among the uses of PM, RM, and KM tools and techniques used in various IT projects. The primary objective of the current chapter was to propose an appropriate research methodology practiced for assessing and examining KM, RM, and PM during the undertaking the IT projects as well as to comprehend by what means KM and RM become a part of PM.

DOI: 10.4018/978-1-5225-8389-9.ch002

INTRODUCTION

The purpose of this study using the qualitative approach was to discover the gap that exists among the uses of PM, RM and KM tools and techniques used in various IT projects. The primary objective of the current chapter was to propose an appropriate research methodology practiced for assessing and examining KM, RM and PM during the undertaking the IT projects as well as to comprehend by what means KM and RM become a part of PM. This chapter focuses on the framework around which research structure is centered. It can be elaborated in terms of research design and rationale followed by role of the researcher. The next segment of this chapter focusses on the justification of utilizing interviews as a primary data collection tool. After this the explanation of data processing and data analysis methodology was used. The last segment elaborates the issues related to trustworthiness and throws light on ethical procedures.

Research Design and Rationale

This study, because of its novel nature, has utilized the qualitative approach and explored the pertinent literature published till the writing of this study with the discussion and analysis of its real-world application facets in different projects. Our research work has been performed successfully by gathering the desired amount of data to meet the research requirements by utilizing available literature assets and sources which include articles, journals and books however in order to complement the research work, the interview sessions with industry professionals was also conducted to utilize as primary source.

The key emphasis of this research work was desk—based study that was successfully conducted first, and then in order to complement it two hundred and seventy interviews were also conducted. These interviews were subsequently used to evaluate and verify the authenticity and validity of research findings to ultimately offer a platform for the purpose of discussion and to propose recommendations. As already discussed in the introduction of chapter 1 that aims and objectives of the research work have been identified in order to outline a route for research / study and to save record of the progress.

Firstly, an extensive review of literature was performed by scrutinizing and exploiting a large amount of secondary sources to collect data and present theories for the purpose of opening study. That had been finalized for the literature of both KM and RM. Numerous sources of information comprising data which were previously been accumulated and accumulated comprising of freely accessible compendium, previously assembled statistical statements as well as reports were exploited to find the sources or causes of risks existing in different stages of the project. They were available in the shape of annual reports, census reports, and industry / business statistical statements, government departments generated reports, international organizations authentic publications like; IMF, ILO, UNO,, WHO, OECD, World Bank, and many other national and international organizations.

Also, RM & KM books, published journals of PMI, published articles of APM, PMBOK, APMBOK, renowned journals of RM & KM covering comprehensive processes and methodologies were analyzed to recognize and scrutinize the RM tools and techniques practiced in different stages of the project that encompassed prevailing systems of "risk matrices"," risk registers", and several other systems. An exhaustive and wide analysis of KM tools and techniques was conducted afterwards by means of exploiting the latest articles as well as recent books for discovering commonalities between KM and RM tools and settings below which the valid techniques of KM can be made applicable to RM.

Furthermore, in order to verify and validate the findings collected through literature review, interview sessions with professionals from project as well as none—project based organizations were scheduled and ultimately conducted to analyze the elements linking to the context of the project. It was made on the findings revealed through the conducted desk- based study that used reports as well as other sources of information as stated previously, for making it systematic and all-inclusive. The foundation for the development of interview template have been created based on these findings. And by utilizing these interview templates the interview sessions were then successfully conducted with highly qualified and experienced professionals in project management appointments operational on diverse projects and these interview sessions were considered adequate to complement a secondary research. It has been explicitly incorporated in the interviews about in what way the project managers handle risks by means of KM practices of "lessons learnt", "brainstorming", and many other practices (that may not be directly obvious to the contributing professionals).

Finally, a comprehensive discussion and analysis built on literature review was carried out, the gathered information gauged and the interview sessions to discover the ways of refining the RM tools and techniques practiced in different stages of the project that shaped a demanding substance to centered the conclusions. It exploited the approaches and strategies of KM as well as RM along with the suggestions and feedback inferred from the interview sessions in conveying the concluding verdict, suggestions and conclusions for upcoming research.

Role of a Researcher

I was acted as an external observer of the organizations whose personnel have been interviewed and had no personal connection with fruitful accomplishment of any of the projects being studied or executed. The researcher partiality was achieved by the process of verification for all data by a "member checking technique". The organizations and members of the project group revised entire amount of data from the research. In the course of retrieving data for the purpose of study, I interviewed management teams and project managers who possessed the potential and authority to affect the data established by the members of the project. The data received from the project developers is likely to be inspired by the delivered information delivered that was provided by the users of the project.

I had the viewpoint that the persons involved in the project shaped their genuineness in the situation. In what way the knowledge was shared in the processes of IT projects was decided by individuals functional in a particular project. As far as my role is concerned I was there to witness the process and comprehend it besides taking or conducting the interview sessions that greatly helped me in determining the authenticity and truthfulness of the statements given by the interwees . I did not try to alter the existing the process, but only witness it. The view of the research was not built on the opinion of the users, project developers, project manager, or any particular stakeholder of the project.

Unit of Analysis

The unit of analysis on the central responding figure of the selected organizations were the General Managers, Managers and Chief Information Officers (CIOs) of the selected organizations operating in different cities of Pakistan like Karachi, Lahore, Islamabad, Peshawar, Faisalabad and Gujranwala Division.

In the context of risk analysis process of IT projects the response from all the senior IT professionals were required for the completion of the study.

Sampling Frame

The sampling frame of this research study encompasses, both public and corporate sector that are listed in services sector of Pakistan. The sampling frame of this study consists of the complete list of companies and the IT professionals who volunteered themselves for interview sessions. The list was obtained from the credible and reliable sources including the complete official addresses and contact information. The list of IT companies were obtained from the website of Pakistan Software Export Board (PSEB), the list of banks operating in Pakistan were downloaded from the official website of State Bank of Pakistan (SBP) and the list of other and the list of other companies included in the sampling frame were collected form the official websites of Karachi, Lahore and Islamabad Stock Exchanges.

A total of 160 companies were initially selected and out of these companies 25 companies were finally shortlisted based on the fact that they are practicing KM Tools & Techniques or in the process of implementing KM Tools & Techniques in the organizations.

Therefore, the sampling frame comprises of 25 companies, both public and corporate sector, operating in Pakistan and practicing or about to implement KM Tools & Techniques include manufacturing industries, banks, software companies, oil and gas, aviation industry etc. Due care was ensured while collecting and selecting data from the credible sources available. As the sampling size or population was quite large, thus initiates the use of an appropriate sampling technique in order to select an appropriate sampling size.

Sampling Technique

Multistage sampling techniques was used which involved random selection of homogeneous group from different companies of Pakistan sectors i.e. IT companies, manufacturing industries, banks etc. . The fraction of IT companies, manufacturing industries, oil and gas, aviation industry and banks was arbitrarily selected for the sample. Then the study respondents were randomly chosen from each of the sectors (Saunders *et al.*, 2011). Based on the previous research studies regarding the selection of sample of companies from the complete sampling frame, percentage values of 8% (Wolfe R.M., 1991; Internal Statistic of Income Service Review, 1999), 10% (US Bureau of Census & US Congress House, 1975; Saxena, R., & Dwivedi, A., 2012), 11% (Internal Statistic of Income Service Review, 1999), 13% (Rosander A. C., 1985), 16% (Internal Statistic of Income Service Review, 1999), 18% (Rehman M., 2003). In order to find an all-inclusive sample size an average fraction value or mean percentage of all scores was accomplished by captivating an average of all the stated percentages. From now, mean percentage came out to be 15%. Based on this 15% of the population or sampling frame of all 160 companies comprising of 80 banks, 65 IT companies, 12 manufacturing industries, 02 oil and gas, and 01 aviation industry were randomly selected in order to gain a representative sample of the organizations. 15% of 160 organizations results in achieving a sample 25 companies from services sectors. The sample size of organization was 25 randomly selected by taking 15% from sampling frame.

For arbitrarily selecting organizations from the list of whole sampling frame of services sectors, Microsoft Office Excel 2013 was utilized to acquire an impartial random selection of the companies permitting to the same size. 25 companies were randomly selected from the list using assigned random numbers until necessary sample size was attained. The comprehensive list of employees was the group of respondents that the study envisioned to simplify to. As a comprehensive list of all the managers employed in services being the population of interest and unit of analysis for the proposed study was inaccessible and very tough to develop a rational and reasonable sampling frame. After classifying the available population of organizational managers, a list of accessible managers was established on personal visit to the organization. Each available manager or responding participant was contacted for interview session in order to ensure the sample representativeness and generalization from the results of entire population. The author Penwarden R. (2013) also advocated that owing to the inaccessibility of the whole list of interview respondent, it was advisable to conduct interview on all the available participants at the given time. This helped minimize the chances of the occurrence of sampling error. According to the "Bosnia-Herzegovina (2001) and Belloni R. (2001), while gathering data from a cluster of respondents with inaccessible and unattainable listing and sampling frame, five visits to an organization were made for conducting interview sessions by randomly selecting. Thus in the current intended study, the survey questionnaires were delivered to the available managers at the time. In order to rise the representation and lessen the researcher error, five visits to each organization were made so that every accessible participant i.e. General Manager, Manager and / or CIO was being reached for interview session in conducive environment.

Demographic Measures

Personnel employed in the services sectors i.e. IT companies, manufacturing industries, oi & gas, aviation industry and banks operative in different cities of Pakistan possessing parallel qualities such as working in the corporate services sectors, performing as IT expert by having technological competences, accountable for the safety and reliability of the serious information of their organization & clients, and competently discharging their duties to provide swift, trustworthy and best services to their clients and other stakeholder by means of high-tech networks. The interview questionnaire had a preliminary section for the details provided for demographic items comprising of age, name of the organization, gender, professional experience. Demographic details also involved status of organization and industrial sector for its operations.

Since the research contributors involved of all managerial employees working in the services sectors arbitrarily selected located in different cities of Pakistan. At the top of interview questionnaire the interviewee has to fill the items related to demographic design of the survey population. In order to differentiate the each of the demographics, each item was given with different options in the questionnaire. Each demographic item was measured on categorical scale in order to gain nominal data responses. First demographic item consisted of the "Gender" with 1 = male and 2 = female. "Age Group" of all managers was segmented into six variations with 1 = 36-40 Years, 2 = 41-45 Years, 3 = 46-50 Years, 4 = 51-55 Years, 5 = 56-60 Years and 6 = 61+ years. "Qualification" included the level of education possessed by the managers. Subsequently, one of the important demographic items was the "Experience". It identified the extent of the time or tenure of employees for serving in the given organization. The last items under the demographic study consisted of "Organization" in which the interwee has to mention the type of organization in which he / she is working.

Research Method

The continuous process for the purpose of research was pursued by the qualitative data collection. It has earlier been elaborated, the first or initial phase involved the review of available literature carried out on the basis of several books, journals and articles on the numerous issues which disturb the project risk as well as its management. Alike KM sources were similarly explored simultaneously to RM for comprehending the extent to which the tools, techniques, methods and approaches of KM can be used. After that the evaluation of reports published by the renowned international organizations as well as publications of government departments were also taken into account for stretched literature review and to discover a shared cluster of risks and its sources experienced by majority of the organizations. By the comprehensions of the associated risks present in different stages of the project currently at hand, the preparation of research questions as well as their categorizations into segments, as declared in the introductory part of the thesis, was arranged. It gives rise to an initial framework having findings for the research study available from secondary sources that was considered sufficient to make the decisions or conclusion. However, in order to develop it further real-world leaning for application in exercise and also to propose relevant real-world suggestions, its verification in the setting of project by means of proper method of primary data research was deemed essential.

The phase of primary data collection may possibly been implemented by numerous ways. The numerous valid choices or options accessible include; case study, method of observation, questionnaires and interviews. The method of observation was rejected as unsuitable as it inherently consumes massive amount of time besides subjectivity which it presents regarding the observations' interpretation (Dhawan *et al.*, 2010) . A research method of case study too needs huge amount of time that was considered limited in this very particular situation. By adopting the case study based approach we are bound to get the results acquired from only one organization in which the case study was performed and the obtained results are inclined towards it (Dhawan *et al.*, 2010). Also, the method of case study is centered on numerous assumptions that may not be considered truthful in all circumstances (Kothari *et al.*, 2004), hence, the selection of this method of primary research was totally phased out.

Lastly, the method of interviews was selected as the method the collection of primary data as additional information in greater depth can be acquired (Dhawan *et al.*, 2010). The Interviews can enquire into investigative and "exploratory questions" dependent on a particular context with an advantage to probe "follow up questions" that are unused if a mail survey by means of questionnaire would have been exercised. The Interviews inherently elude misinterpretations by accordingly adjusting the language to the level of aptitude or education of the individual who is being interviewed (Dhawan *et al.*, 2010). Furthermore, it includes the method of observation that can be made applicable to the oral or verbal replies to many questions (Dhawan *et al.*, 2010). To grip this and get existing in-depth comprehension, semi-structured interviews were decided to be the finest choice. This guaranteed that an identical information has been gathered however it still permissible for a definite extent of freedom in order to adjust to the context and to make suitable to the current situation and state of an interviewee. That makes it informal to acquire personal information (implied in some cases) that is usually considered tough to acquire by means of questionnaires or any other standard or medium (Dhawan *et al.*, 2010) and opposition to replying few questions could be catered with proper exercise of interviewer's expertise and skills (Punch *et al.*, 2005).

The approach considered face-to-face interviews however due to different geographical sites of the people to be interviewed few of the interviews sessions were conducted via telephone that still preserves the personal contact between the interviewer and the respondent. In order to ensure superior handling and dealing of the questions and the circumstances as well, the interview sessions were steered by the author personally while shunning any sort of partiality which could perhaps effect outcomes or results. This smoothed as an author possesses the thorough understanding of the significance and the study's background. The next phase was of conducting or arranging the interviews as a "data-gathering method" for qualitative research. It was followed by the stress on the methods of "analysis description", and understanding interpretation of interview data as chunk of a process.

Interviews for the Purpose of Data Collection

The interviews or interview sessions were required as they have inherent capacity to perform as a foundation source to get primary data which can complement the secondary data being analyzed in the "desk-based" study. They were, still, applied in a further positive instead of exploratory way as chunk of qualitative research. This aided in added confirmatory research with a practical combination of primary and secondary research. The total number of ten interviews were arranged and conducted. The rationale or justification for these interviews is elucidated in the next section.

Rationale of Interview

The first and foremost facet that need consideration or to put emphasis on, soon after justifying and finishing interview sessions as the source of primary data, a rationale was required to set for them. The necessity was to get confirmation and more to grow the issues elevated by means of a secondary research. As the data collected from the secondary sources, in the shape of reports and publications of different international organizations, they had encompassed or covered the entire range of projects from across the world in miscellaneous fields, a comparable feature was essential to shape the interviews also. Accordingly, the interview sessions needed employees from diverse IT project domains with solid and proven experience in the field of PM.

Thus, the interviewees were carefully chosen on the rationale like that their skills and proficiency varied in different industries. The extreme acute criterion for the selection of interviewee was having solid practical skills and experience in the domains of KM as well as in RM. The interviewee or respondents were chosen carefully on the base of their professional portfolio that encompassed their appointments i.e. Team Leaders, Project, Program and Portfolio Managers. The total number of 270 interviews were arranged and conducted that traversed through diverse businesses or industries. The sample size is calculated by using the formula;

Sample Size = (Z-score)^2*SD*(1-SD)/ (margin of error) = 270.

(Confidence Level 90%, SD = 0.5, Margin of error +/- 5%)

The taken sampling figure was considered sufficient as it comprised entire range of information being watched for and incorporated all the criteria needed for the conduct of interviews as a tool of primary research. It is being willingly admitted an acknowledged that there exists restrictions / limitations and boundaries integral in such type of study but as the interviews were supposed to be exploited to support the "desk-based" study, this figure was considered adequate. Furthermore, as the primary research is not utilized for claiming any statistical importance to the findings or outcomes, henceforward no effort is extended to present the organizations or respondents as statistically illustrative or representative, nor any statistical generalizations were inferred. However even then the obtained results are greatly valid as these results are made on the findings obtained from the secondary research while confirming and validating these results from primary research.

Objectives of Interview

The reason to conduct interviews was divided or segmented into goals and objectives which develop an aim for steering these goals and objectives clearly. As declared earlier, the interview template as the research gadget was founded on the findings from Phase-1 of this study i.e. the secondary research. The goals and objectives were well-defined from the topic in hand and the research questions that ascended from the secondary data which contained the organizations project reports of WHO, UN, UNESCO, OECD, World Bank and others. The template was polished to make it as specific and brief as thinkable. The objectives are as follows:

- To understand and analyze the level of KM in the organization and the tools being used
- To understand and analyze the level of RM in the organization and the tools being used
- To verify and validate risks of different stages of IT project as investigated and examined by the secondary research and analyze their deepness
- To comprehend the interviewee's viewpoint on the similarities between the KM and RM and endorse the ones originated in the research
- To obtain the interviewee's feedback on the integration of KM into RM and recommendations for upgrading of both RM and KM and their joint functioning

Methodology for Interview

The interview pursued a semi-structured approach instead of fully structured which concentrated it elasticity to shape to the context. This approach is appropriate as the sequence and language of the questions may be custom-made during the interview (Punch *et al.*, 2007). In, the semi-structured arrangement of the interview, the interviewer may reply questions to make clarifications for acquiring superior replies. Depending on the information being retrieved, fresh questions according to the feedback of the interviewee were shaped leading to an impartial discussion and endorsement of the objectives. This lessens flexibility in contrast of interviews, but does not confine the study as the data acquired will not be exploited for the sake of comparison. Furthermore, this offers extra liberty while the replies are recorded to contain pertinent aspects and eliminate the ones that may appear unsuitable (Kothari *et al.*, 2004).

The interview was also supplemented by open-ended questions in the interview template which were built on the findings initiated in the research. This means the interview was not restricted on just the questions provided or the choices available. This solidified freedom in modifying the questions according to the context of the circumstances and providing an open framework for intensive, conversational, two-way communication. The questions followed an order within the template which possesses a combination of scaled response as well as standardized open ended questions. The interviews were piloted in person or over the telephone in few cases. Each and every interview took around 45-60 minutes to conduct. The process of the analysis of information acquired both form the primary and secondary sources is elucidated in the next chapter. The methodology adopted for the research work is depicted in Figure 1.

Trustworthiness Issues

Although the author of (Yin *et al.*, 2013) recommended that inner validity was chunk of the data analysis of an exploratory case study. Triangulation among the observation, documents and interviews was utilized to authenticate the information about the projects that were achieved from this research. In, (Yin *et al.*, 2013) the author have deliberated different types of triangulation comprising dissimilar methods for triangulation and diverse theories. He

Figure 1. Research methodology

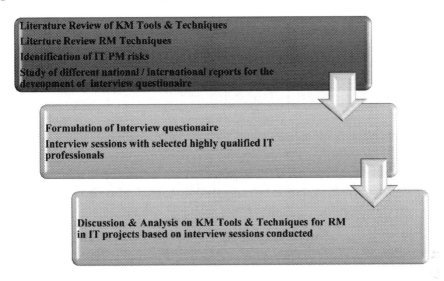

remarks that the data source method used in this research will reinforce the legitimacy. The author (Maxwell *et al.*,2005) pointed out that triangulation did not always rise credibility. All the sources of data could be partial and may not be authenticated. Triangulation was utilized to thwart unfairness of the information gathered and offer rightful information for the research. By matching unlike projects in the organization, the credibility of the research will increase. Another significant concern for the credibility of study was the amount of time required to be spent in the field. For this study, I spent four months working with the project team members, team leaders, project managers, program managers and portfolio managers. This was an acceptable amount of time at diverse industries to acquire trustworthy data from the research.

Credibility was desirable for authenticating the information inside the organization, and transferability was desirable to generalize the research and relate it to organizations external of the one being studied. Transferability has boundaries in qualitative research. The authors (Lincoln *et al.*, 2011) mentioned that the researcher does not know the particulars about the project setting to which the research was being shifted. Without having the meaningful details regarding the project marks any claims about generalization or transferability to another project untrustworthy. To increase the research transferability, the authors have (Lincoln *et al.*, 2011) suggested that the face-to-face interview provide a methodological report. The methodological report for this research encompassed a comprehensive account of the methods, measures and investigator utilized in the research.

Ethical Methods and Procedures

The research elaborate an industrial sector and individuals that are working on IT projects for their respective organization. To promise the ethical handling of the organization and the individuals a (a) letter of cooperation for working with the organization, (b) letter of consent for piloting interviews and (c) letter of confidentiality for all information acquired during the course of the research.

A letter of cooperation was desired before the conducted of any type of research work with the project team members, team leader, project managers, the management of respective organization and the agreement of other stakeholders is desired. The letter of cooperation for working with the organization encompassed the recruitment process, collection of data, and activities related to dissemination of activities that will happen at the site. An agreement form for conducting interviews and research comprised the research procedure and few interview questions that were included in the research. The authors (Lincoln *et al.*, 2011) point out that although permission is delivered, this does not guarantee that the interviewee has decided to being openly cited in the research. The authors (Patton *et al.*,2002) deliberated that during the course of interviews the information will be exposed by the interviewee that was not intentional. There were ethical boundaries in the information that is to be exploited for the research and those fears were chunk of the research. A letter of consent was utilized to guarantee the information collected from the research will not be revealed to the public and to not unveil the contributor's confidential information that was portion of the research. The process to apprentice individuals encompassed in the research was in collaboration with the respective organization. The respective organization nominated project team members and project managers that were interviewed during the research. The data composed from the research was made confidential. The data will be held personally by me in encrypted files on a password protected computer. The data will likely to be smashed in 3 years' time. Information was delivered to the respective organization and other involved groups without disclosing the contributors identity while giving the information. There were not any perks or incentives for interviews for the research. The interviews were totally confidential and voluntary. The sample population being studied was fit and healthy grown person well over 35 years of age.

REFERENCES

Collins, J. C. (2001). *Good to great: Why some companies make the leap—and others don't*. New York: Harper Business.

Conley, C. A., & Zheng, W. (2009). Factors Critical to Knowledge Management Success. *Advances in Developing Human Resources, 11*(3), 334-348. doi:10.1177/1523422309338159

Cox, A. (2005). What are communities of practice? A comparative review of four seminal works. *Journal of Information Science, 31*(6), 527–540. doi:10.1177/0165551505057016

Dey, P. K. (2010). Managing project risk using combined analytic hierarchy process and risk map. *Applied Soft Computing, 10*, 990-1000. doi:10.1016/j.asoc.2010.03.010

Dhawan, S. (2010). *Research Methodology for Business and Management Studies*. Delhi: Global Media.

Drucker, P. F. (1977). *An Introductory View of Management*. Newport: Harper's College Press.

Emblemsvåg, J. (2010). The augmented subjective risk management process. *Management Decision, 48*(2), 248-259. doi:10.1108/00251741011022608

Farias, L. L., Travassos, G. H., & Rocha, A. R. (2003). Managing Organizational Risk Knowledge. *Journal of Universal Computer Science, 9*(7), 670–681.

Franke, A. (1987). Risk analysis in project management. *International Journal of Project Management, 5*(1), 29–34. doi:10.1016/0263-7863(87)90007-X

Fugate, B. S., Stank, T. P., & Mentzer, J. T. (2009). *Linking improved knowledge management to operational and organizational performance. Journal of Operations Management, 27(3)*, 247–264. doi:10.1016/j.jom.2008.09.003

Herremans, I. M., Isaac, R. G., Kline, T. J. B., & Nazari, J. A. (2011). Intellectual Capital and Uncertainty of Knowledge: Control by Design of the Management System. *Journal of Business Ethics, 98*(4), 627-640. doi:10.100710551-010-0642-7

Holtshouse, D. (1999). Ten Knowledge Domains–Model of a Knowledge-Driven Company? *Knowledge and Process Management.*

Chapter 3
Analysis and Results

ABSTRACT

This chapter makes available the analysis of collected information for the sole reason of research. It has been prepared for the conduct of secondary research that shapes an appropriate way for the purpose of primary research framework. Then the information collected by virtue of several conducted interviews was examined and analyzed. Hence, the chapter develops the basis of the platform on which the discussion is founded. In the last section of this chapter, the authors presented the trustworthiness of evidence of their research work.

DOI: 10.4018/978-1-5225-8389-9.ch003

INTRODUCTION

The sole purpose of this research work was to comprehend the part of KM and RM in projects. To achieve this goal, I personally investigated, inspected and analyzed the usage of KM tools and techniques in PM. This research work documented and acknowledged the progression of the tools and techniques of PM have considered parallel with the tools and techniques of KM in order to decide at what place they can be pooled to increase the performance level of the projects related with IT. The author's research work also documented, acknowledged and evaluated the usage of KM in IT PM in diverse industrial sector. This was anticipated that the outcome and result of this analytical work would have noteworthy implications, both from an organizational and strategic standpoint, for prospective projects.

The dominant research question addresses how KM is used in the PM process of an IT section of an organization. KM is a central part of the PM process, and there are several theories about the usage of KM in the organizations of diverse structure. As far as this research work is concerned, I endeavored to collect information about KM in the PM process for different organizations located in different cities of Pakistan.

Instead of studying the individual projects in the organizations, I decided to interview the highly qualified IT professionals working and possesses extensive knowledge and experience in five different operational / business areas of the IT domain and the IT projects that were being constructed or developed. Each of the operational / business area encompassed projects, and no project has a privilege to cross the boundaries of operational / business area. One of the operational / business areas only applies a predictive process for the development of systems, and other three applied an adaptive approach. The correction of issues related to the existing system is being operated by another IT area.

SETTINGS FOR RESEARCH

The contributors in this research were IT project stakeholders involved in the development and commissioning of projects for their respective organization ranging from Oil & Gas to Manufacturing Firms. The IT project stakeholders were deeply involved and busy in five dissimilar project areas of their respective organization. The IT project stakeholders comprised (a) project team members, (b) project, program and portfolio managers, and (c) clients linked with IT projects. A small number participants were my classmates at a local university whom I met in the past 15 years, but I did not get an opportunity to converse with them for a long time and did not informally question them to become a part of my research. The General Managers IT or equivalent at the organizations recommended the contributors or participants, but the contribution or participation was entirely voluntary. Every contributor or participant volunteered for interview received an introductory e-mail from my side that arranged and settled the interview session.

Demographics

The contributors or participants in this research work all operated for their respective organization at a good position and enjoys good rapport among their peers and seniors. This obligation was chunk of the agreement with all the organizations involved for the research work. The contributors or participants were considered as the project team members, project clients or managers. The contributors or participants had been with the organization for more than 11 years. There were not the same numbers of male and female members in the research. Although the members in the research often conversed with people outside of Pakistan, all of the contributors worked in Pakistan. The detailed demographic analysis has been depicted in Table 1.

Similarly, the descriptive frequencies of interview questionnaire items have been determined using an SPSS statistical software. The descriptive frequencies of the interview questions have been summarized in Table 2.

Also, in order to enhance the reliability of the research work the reliability analysis of the variables have been carried out to ascertain the reliability of independent variables (Table 3).

Since, the reliability of each chosen independent variable is greater than 0.7 that depicts a decent level of reliability and it also reveals that if the study conducted under the same conditions the results would likely to be identical.

The estimates of correlation have been given in Table 4.

From Table 4 we can infer that all the independent variables have positive correlation with dependent variable (Risk Analysis of IT Projects).

Analysis and Results

Table 1. Demographic frequencies of the respondents

Category	Percentage	Frequency
Gender		
Male	32.5%	65
Female	67.5%	135
Age Group		
36-40 years	12.5%	25
41-45 years	32.5%	65
46-50 year	45.0%	90
51-55 years	10.0%	20
Qualification		
Bachelor's 14 years	5.0%	10
Bachelor's 16 years	56.0%	112
Master's 16 years	24.0%	48
Master's 18 years	15.0%	30
Experience		
11-15 years	64.0%	128
16-20 years	21.0%	42
21-25 years	12.0%	24
26-30 years	3.0%	06
Type of Organization		
Public Sector Company	43.0%	86
Private Limited Company	57.0%	114

Table 2. Descriptive Frequencies of Independent Variables

Variables	Minimum	Maximum	Mean	Std. Dev
CoP	2	6	3.479	.214
KD	4	6	5.493	.096
LL	3	6	4.507	.130
BS	4	6	5.554	.089
KMaps	4	6	5.495	.062
KA	4	6	5.561	.077
BM	0	5	2.438	.398
ST	3	6	4.013	.134
RW	3	6	4.507	.130
CPL	4	6	5.554	.089
AAR	2	6	3.479	.214
KF	4	6	5.493	.096

Table 3. Reliability of independent variables

Variables	Cron Batch Alpha
CoP	0.707
KD	0.718
LL	0.706
BS	0.745
KMaps	0.758
KA	0.805
BM	0.812
ST	0.742
RW	0.786
CPL	0.767
AAR	0.765
KF	0.803

Table 4. Estimates of correlation analysis

Variable	CoP	KD	LL	BS	KMaps	KA	BM	ST	RW	CPL	AAR	KF
CoP	1.0	0.75	0.85	0.68	0.76	0.97	0.65	0.56	0.63	0.75	0.78	0.87
KD	0.66	1.0	0.67	0.78	0.86	0.75	0.73	0.64	0.69	0.70	0.86	0.73
LL	0.74	0.76	1.0	0.65	0.72	0.68	0.59	0.75	0.86	0.92	0.75	0.65
BS	0.85	0.68	0.76	1.0	0.75	0.73	0.64	0.69	0.70	0.86	0.73	0.75
KMaps	0.75	0.73	0.64	0.69	1.0	0.75	0.85	0.68	0.76	0.97	0.65	0.56
KA	0.69	0.70	0.86	0.73	0.75	1.0	0.65	0.72	0.68	0.59	0.75	0.65
BM	0.75	0.85	0.68	0.76	0.97	0.75	1.0	0.72	0.68	0.59	0.75	0.72
ST	0.65	0.72	0.68	0.59	0.75	0.86	0.65	1.0	0.64	0.69	0.70	0.86
RW	0.65	0.72	0.68	0.75	0.86	0.92	0.75	0.75	1.0	0.72	0.68	0.59
CPL	0.65	0.72	0.68	0.56	0.67	0.68	0.63	0.58	0.57	1.0	0.54	0.66
AAR	0.68	0.76	0.97	0.86	0.65	0.86	0.86	0.73	0.75	0.77	1.0	0.74
KF	0.63	0.58	0.57	0.72	0.68	0.59	0.85	0.68	0.76	0.65	0.63	1.0

Furthermore, as the p value of each independent variable, as depicted in Table 5, is less than 0.05, so we can say that the conceptual framework is valid.

Table 6 shows that 82% change is occurring in dependent variable due to independent variable which is a major change of independent variables in IT risk management. 82% is a significant change.

Table 7 depicts that by the increase of one unit of each independent variable there is an increase occur in consumer buying behavior.

Analysis of Secondary Data

This section of the chapter uses the statements and reports of international organizations and companies besides the problems and issues highlighted

Table 5. Independent variables 'p' value

Variables	P Value
CoP	0.02
KD	0.01
LL	0.00
BS	0.014
KMaps	0.017
KA	0.012
BM	0.019
ST	0.023
RW	0.025
CPL	0.034
AAR	0.028
KF	0.024

Table 6. Regression Analysis

Model Summary				
Model	R	R Square	Adjusted R Square	Std. Error of the Estimate
1	0.820	0.673	0.633	0.76355

Table 7. Coefficients

Model		Unstandardized Coefficients		Standardized Coefficients	t	Sig.
		B	Std. Error	Beta		
1	(Constant)	13.246	2.545		5.216	0.000
	CoP	0.215	0.104	0.107	2.051	0.042
	KD	0.131	0.998	0.065	1.305	0.195
	LL	0.143	0.097	0.88	1.454	0.146
	BS	0.563	0.087	0.389	6.576	0.000
	KMaps	0.387	0.082	0.241	4.763	0.000
	KA	0.143	0.097	0.88	1.454	0.146
	BM	0.563	0.087	0.389	6.576	0.000
	ST	0.131	0.998	0.065	1.305	0.195
	RW	0.387	0.082	0.241	4.763	0.000
	CPL	0.215	0.104	0.107	2.051	0.042
	AAR	0.131	0.998	0.065	1.305	0.195
	KF	0.132	0.997	0.066	1.307	0.197

in numerous articles published in renowned journal to offer the analysis of a secondary research acquired by means of stretched literature review. At the first instance the analysis of secondary data is considered extremely vital as it projects many relevant areas that required to be confirmed and verified by virtue of a primary research done in the shape of several conducted interview sessions. While performing this, the analysis reviews the investigation process of the key sources of the risks which is considered as the first and foremost objective which initiates when the project is commenced and occur at different stages of the project. The next sub-section elaborates the analysis of secondary data.

Sources of Risks Occurred at Different Stages of the Project

Such sources of risks are considered as the boundaries and these boundaries originate during different stages of an IT project such as the planning stage, execution stage etc. (Farias *et al.*,2003). As section 2.2 of the research completed on RM, the nature of such sources are "epistemic" i.e. these sources are linked to some level of uncertainty concerning the knowledge about things which shapes the concentration of the current section in discussion. Such types of risks are inherently possess the "dynamic nature" because such types of risks alter or vary over a period of time as the obtainability and accessibility of precise and detailed information is increased. The genuine uncertainty does not lie in the risk itself however it in turn directs towards it. As an uncertainty of a certain extent arises because a certain amount of information is deficient, the number of risks that are under consideration ascend because of the decisions taken in that particular circumstances. A group of such sources of risks has obtained and collected through several organization that operate at international level or globally in order to increase the comprehension level of the problem.

The KM process begins at knowledge generation stage that overlaps the proposal stage of project. The entire amount of information is necessary be in obvious format or shape, so that it can be placed in relevant documents. Due to expectations of stakeholders and principal assumptions, that are available in unstated shape or format till this stage, they are to be placed as contractual terms and project scope has to be defined. Hence, this paved the way for the process of externalization. The key problems come across during several project stages which developed as risks' sources originated in this research are elaborated under:

Non-Availability of Information

World Health Organization (WHO) by virtue of experience of dynamic and diverse nature of its undertaken multi-billion dollar projects have acknowledged that the knowledge generation process synstudyis slow as well as costly(Antik *et al.*,2007). Because of the fact that this development is costly, few facets of knowledge generation process would be eliminated or not taken into consideration which ultimately guides towards the deficiency of desired information. As concerns to its sluggish nature, there can be either low or no access to pertinent information because of the vagueness about knowledge being created by the time it is needed or necessary. Therefore, there exists a gap or discontinuity between the available and expected sources of information (UNESCO 2009). The theorist, Mayor in 2010 elaborates it as "The gap between an actual situation or the perception of it and the required or expected situation". Also, the above mentioned problem of discontinuity or gap is magnified due to the absence or lack of knowledge sharing, exclusively among the project team players as well as other stakeholders of the project.

Lack of a Commonly Defined Context

This step is considered as a first and foremost step in RM process as previously elaborated in the literature review section. The level of uncertainty lies in the background of projects is basically the deficiency of information which is obvious as the mark difference between the desired and available information in order to carry out a specific activity (Antvik *et al.*, 2007). Inserting a process of describing the cooperative context inside the organizational culture is considered thought-provoking however required work (Baaldeon *et al.*, 2008). However even to date, the organizations tumble into the deception of project execution, fails to make a diagnosis regarding the importance of generating a mutual context on the foremost instance. It is partially considered as a consequence of limited project budget as well as schedules and agendas heading towards scarcity of collaborative communication among the users and producers of the information. This collaboration or interaction can help in determining the origins of present data / information by means of tools used for "knowledge mapping" and many others. This can support by the methods of retrieving them, assessing various assumptions as well as needs of the varied project stakeholders and after that distributing it among all that leads to a joint and common information pool.

The context established at this very stage is considered as a challenge as it constructs wide-ranging interpretations however the progression to the shared context progresses headed for attaining the goals of KM and RM. Also, setting up of mutual context helps in a proof of identity of risks as well as the competencies of an organization. A "SWOT analysis" explains this by replacing the assumed risks with threats and opportunities as well as the competencies of organizations for strengths and weaknesses [18]. An information audit can be revealed by a knowledge SWOT in this research.

Insufficient Flow of Information

The another major contributing source of risk in the IT project which head towards the growth of risks is basically the inadequate drift of information that confines the "knowledge spiral" process as the conducted literature review already elaborated it. That particular source of risk differs during the execution of various projects on which the organizations even the well-established organizations reliant on the deepness of KM that is currently in practice as the primary research made it obvious. The dearth of required information coupled with the low flow of information among the diverse teams as well as persons demonstrate them as hindrances and come to be obvious by virtue of their effects that are of obstructive nature (Mabu et al 2013) .

The final and resultant effect of that controlled flow is a limited synergy created amongst the initiatives in use that are not line up with one another and may originate clashes. Also, that can take to incapacity in respect of the entire range of involved variables and factors compulsory to make a correct decision . The management of risk is reliant on a repeated flowing of data / information via various departments of an organization. The reason for managing a stream of information is to support teams as well as individuals to make better decisions which is crucial for heading the projects to success.

Absence of Mutual Framework Reference

While performing projects of various nature in different countries across the globe, the World Health Organization (WHO) had estimated that there lies a nonexistence of mutual framework required for the translation and transfer of knowledge (WHO 2013). Because of this lack of reference, there exists no uniformity in the made assumptions and rigorously carried analysis of various sections or departments of the organization and the individuals possessing a knowledge. It is in turn a deficiency of an identical organization extensive RM approach. Even at the United Nations (UN) this fact is obvious. The diverse and peculiar methodologies are being employed even at UN level by its various departments and programs based on current RM standards and practices. Consequently, there exists a dearth of consistency in the processes which guides to different approaches for the purpose of identification, evaluation, reporting of risks and replying to the risks in the very same project over dissimilar project stages (UN 2012).

Also, even inside such approaches there exists a dearth of integration concerning the qualitative and quantitative analysis methods as the conducted literature review already elucidated it in the earlier parts of the research work. Due to the rise in nonstop inventions and innovations, distribution of knowledge and the concepts of "learning-by-doing", there exists a dire requirement to create broad and common framework to seal the "know-do-hole" simultaneously by means of available systems in order to deal with them . This outcomes in improving an ability to make knowledgeable decisions or pick choices based on knowledge. By means of a mutual framework, all the tasks come under the umbrella of shared framework heading towards the operations' integration process across the entire organization making obvious the entire range of known risks to all the project stakeholders therefore improving the level of transparency, accountability and hence performance.

Unproductive Linkage Arrangements or Systems

It is considered as one of the multifaceted difficulties ascending from the initial stages of IT projects prepared seeming by UNESCO, a renowned international organization. It has been discovered by UNESCO that rare information pooled with poor network arrangements or systems confines a creation and the development of connections and links exist between dissimilar domains of knowledge (UNESCO 2009). It is primarily initiated from the fact that the data and information is available in distributed shapes across the entire organization. Diverse systems are being utilized by various sections or departments of organization that are not well-matched with one another therefore heading towards the complexity in implementing common actions and coordinated decisions. The technological structures of complicated arrangement does not encourage the cooperation on intersectional basis. That is pretty serious in the dynamic and vibrant environment of an IT project that demands a requirement for an integrated approach to carry out the analysis of data and information. The Information & Communication Technology contributes as a key player by aiding as a medium for information assembly and also as distribution points that may be of more assistance in engineering a system or network for connecting the entire range of inaccessible areas of knowledge areas into a single combined network.

Rapid Technological Change

Every person living in this world who possesses even a little knowledge about computers and IT must agree with the "fact" that the development in computer industry is extremely rapid. This rapid change in the realm of Information Technology can contribute to an indefinite extent at which the IT project experience fiasco. This can be justified by saying that if an organization starts to develop a software application for a local hospital that helps the doctors to know about the medical history of a patient by using a specific software platform. All of a sudden, if the developer of the chosen software platform stops to provide updates for the chosen software platform then the project will likely to stuck somewhere in the middle of the project and eventually that not only brings bad rapport to the organization but also results in colossal financial losses.

Financial Constraints

Everybody knows that nothing comes for free in this world and the IT projects are no exception. In order to ensure the timely completion and delivery of the project the organization undertaking an IT project must ensure during the planning phase of the project that sufficient amount of capital is at the disposal of the project manager. In case the allocated funds cannot be transferred to the project manager then the project manager must have a contingency plan to immediately get out of this "mess" without disrupting normal pace of the project.

Security Risks

The security risks are also attached with the IT projects. There always lies a breach of information by the person(s) involved in the project. If the confidential information pertaining to the development of software / IT project is shared with the employee of rival organization then that causes unmeasurable amount of loss.

Human Resources Risk

The risk associated with human resources as far as IT project are concerned can be devastating. Once the president of IBM (International Business Machine) said that "if somebody takes all the belongings of the IBM and we only left with the people who are currently working in IBM, I will make the IBM of even bigger stature within few years". From the quoted saying it is evident that human resource is the precious all the available resources and if skillful and talented people leave the organization then the consequences can easily be realized.

Risk of Success

IT project are subject to the success risk. This type of risk happens when the project is such a huge success that it started to draw extra transactions than it was expected to draw and flops to scale Analysis and Results to excess requirement(s).

Analysis of Primary Data

By virtue of the sources or origins of risks obvious after the secondary data has been analyzed, it considered mandatory to configure the sources of risks into segments of questions for the purpose of authentication by virtue of interview sessions to endorse their presence and magnitude. That was arranged in a shape of an interview template, as an instrument of research, which was utilized for each and every interview session. It enclosed all the questions that are required to be explored. The analysis will be revealed in the forthcoming paragraphs.

Processing of Data

The first and foremost step after gathering of raw data with the help of interviews was the process of data and content analysis. Due to this reason, labor-intensive coding using both MS Excel and MS Word besides several paper copies was utilized. For qualitative analysis computer software packages were utilized. Quite often, the descriptions of the research methods are fastened in the researchers affirming the practice of NVIVO, SPSS or any other available software tool for the data analysis.

Analysis of Content

As the nature of the interviews are semi-structured and instead of structured, more emphasis was put on the approach of content analysis to make sensible and figure out seeming themes. This was executed through editing that guaranteed the uniformity, consistency and accuracy of data (Kothari *et al.*, 2004). This was pursued by 'Field Editing' (Kothari *et al.*, 2004). which appraised the information acquired. As the interviews were used for endorsement related to the findings of the desk-based study and to get expressive feedback about the desired results, inferences were made from the composed facts through the process of analytic induction which mark out concepts (Punch *et al.*,2005) and lastly scripting down of summaries with outlining the relevant areas that are to be consumed in the dissertation. To analyze a wider significance of research findings, interpretations were developed through the illumination of descriptive concepts which are elaborated in the analysis and discussion chapter. These inferences elucidate the researcher's observations and remarks while giving theoretical conceptions.

Process of Interpretation

The interpretation process as portion of the analytic induction, that shapes the foundation for the analysis of content, has been applied in different steps. Firstly, the facts and points which were liable to subjectivity and connected to a specific context has been ruled out (Punch *et al.*,2005). Also, the descriptions of associations between varied sets of data have been figured out. Furthermore, the complete range of related associations of the findings with one another were interconnected to discover a "coherent theme" (Taylor *et al.*, 2008). This made a framework for the analysis that is to be used in the discussion section besides the secondary data. Lastly, precise consideration has been rewarded to the fact to retain a persistent distinction on the goals and objectives all the interview sessions conducted and also to theoretical conceptions from the sources of secondary data. This process of interpretation has been achieved once the deliberation of all important factors that disturb the context to escape deceitful generalization has been carried out (Taylor *et al.*, 2008).

The interviews' analysis was organized in a systematic approach to develop sequence and accepting as chunk of the content analysis (Dhawan *et al.*,2008). Due to this purpose, a summary for every interview was established that integrated the open ended, suggestive and multiple choice questions. The analysis was completed in five different steps i.e.:

1. Data evaluation, answers and results acquired
2. Focus on topic and purpose of evaluation
3. Patterns and themes identification and the establishment of an abstract
4. Endorsement and confirmation of secondary data
5. Use for discussion and to make conclusion

Removal of Subjectivity and Biasness

The process of interpretation has been utilized using appropriate examination to evade any subjectivity and biasness. The interpretation process steps that were used in the previous section elucidates it. As depicted in the interview template, an entire range of variables for the analysis (regardless of their standing estimated by the conducted literature review) was incorporated to reject the consequences of design subjectivity and biasness. In reality, it is considered almost impractical to generate flawless as well as impartial instrument of research (such as template used for Interview purposes) no matter to what extreme extent the efforts made in this condition to endorse the findings. But the interview template was autonomously analyses by my fellow colleague at College of Aeronautical Engineering, NUST to uproot any biasness and was reviewed numerous times before settling to the conclusive version. It paid precise consideration to the linguistics and dialects of the questions to discourage any partiality and chauvinism that could lead the replies in a specific direction as well as to avoid any influential wording. The moderator biasness has evaded by maintaining neutrality and not providing peculiar opinions and views during the interview session with the candidate.

The interviews created few results that were not consistent with the other part of the available set of data. These have been analyzed but were not given emphasis to evade deceitful generalization and therefore are not depicted as noteworthy. The recurrent theme only and the results in the shape of sources or origins of risks which have been endorsed by primary research was utilized for discussion and analysis. Also, the entire literature review, contents of research, findings and discussion of the research have been peer reviewed by three autonomous individuals in order to preserve impartiality.

The findings fetched out from the pool of primary data are summarized in the subsequent section. The recurrent theme and suggestions is then pursued that was utilized besides the secondary information taken from the conducted literature review for the purpose discussion and analysis.

Analysis of Confirmations and Primary Research Based Suggestions

Through the analysis and scrutiny of the literature review, the dominant theme regarding risks and the methodology to the available primary data, the template for interview was shaped and interview sessions were arranged and conducted. The main outcomes revealed from the summaries of each of the interview session conducted are given below. This defines the recurrent endorsement of the literature review which makes obvious the entire theme, the main outlines of which are segmented into five segments as consumed in the interview template (See Appendix). The final segment too elucidates the recommendations from the interviewees for the amalgamation of KM and RM. The analyzed segmented content is elaborated below:

Level of KM and RM in Organizations

There exists an evolving theme of progressively developing KM that is gently piercing into the organizational (project as well as business) strategy through agendas in industries and organizations. This is emerging in the shape of bond of "Social Networks" for casually distributing experiences. For its assistance and facilitation, there exists a certain level of transparency in organizations with horizontal hierarchical structure to make liberal recommendations and suggestions environment with open door policy to swiftly convert and transform ideas into effective decisions.

As far as RM is concerned, both small and big organizations endeavor to bring up to date the "SWOT analysis" at every stage of the project being undertaken to line up the tasks and assignments to the project goals and objectives. There exists a mutual goal which the organizations need to attain that is to practice KM at organizational level and RM at project level along with their optimal alliance and collaboration.

Risks Verification at Different Stages of the Project

The interviewees were all in accord concerning the risks depicted in section 4.1. The absence or non-availability of information was deliberated to be the greatest dominant source of risk. This is expanded with the risk of insufficient flow of information. This necessitates the strategic and organizational process structures to be knowledge beneficial sharing with the consequence of COP's at intra as well as inter project level. There comes a necessity for like structures for all projects due to the dearth of mutual framework of reference. This can be aided with structured and defined steps for project to assist flow of work needing least instruction and efforts, therefore decreasing 'Reinventing the wheel' while reducing workload and augmenting profitability.

Likenesses Between KM and RM Approaches

On the similarities front, both KM and RM use assemblies in the form of Kick off meetings for the purpose ice breaking with internal stakeholders, project teams, contractors, external consultants, and others. Both the domains demand the requirement for taking into account all the stakeholders (internal as well as external) strategic partners. Both need the application of KM support system instead of their mere formation with the autonomy at personal levels for taking decisions. There is a simple requirement to improve the acceptance of knowledge and distribution in all directions to improve efficiency:

RECOMMENDATIONS FOR INTEGRATION OF KM INTO RM

It has been suggested by bulk of interviewees that at the project level, collaboration with partners and external consultants for 'Benchmarking' purpose is necessary to employ it for 'GAP' analysis to attain suitable knowledge mapping. The use of concepts like 'Peer Network' for knowledge sharing where young and junior employees deliberate and absorb from experiences one can be of benefited both at the project as well as organizational level. The recurring feedback has been of presenting the flexible approach for handling changes. For this purpose, the project methods and procedures to be developed must be flexible; dependent on the size and complexity of project i.e.

- **For "SMALL" Projects:** Less difficult tools, techniques, approaches needed, personalized formats and templates, decision making at individual level etc.
- **For "BIG" Projects:** Standard and specialized tools, techniques, a framework to initiate extra impact and grip complexity, formal or official approaches and equally shared formats and templates.

With the assistance of findings from the conducted literature review and interviews it is promising to move forward to a thorough discussion about the second, third, fourth and fifth (last) objective, as elaborated in the next chapter.

Evidence of Trustworthiness

It is the amount to which one has sureness in the findings of the research. To rise the sureness in the research findings, the responses to questions were decided to be trustworthy by having more than one interviewee give the identical reply. Other interviews certified the responses for each individual's interview. The interviewee endorsed the transcripts for their interview. The endorsement by others and the authentication of the transcript offer evidence of the trustworthiness of the research.

Credibility

As part of the 10 interviews, the findings of the interviews were confirmed and authenticated with extra comments. The triangulation has been added by this process. During the process of interviewing, the findings were steady or consistent.

Transferability

Although this research was based on the IT PM processes involving the integration of KM and RM in diverse organizations, the analysis gives a foundation for more research in organizations located outside Pakistan. The results of this research may be shifted to other organizations that consist of project teams with settings like to our considered organization. Other organizations that possesses the similar structure of clients and project teams and that were participated with this research may be attracted in getting the results of this research. Numerous organizations are involved in IT related projects and are consuming the existing PM model that does not emphasis on KM and RM, and this research could be significant.

Dependability

For the reliability and dependability of the research, this research delivered sufficient information on the process and information establish in the research for the purpose audit inquiry. The audit with good-quality voice recordings and field notes of the interviews form the research trustworthy.

Conformability

Conformability is presented by the validation of the information by other persons. In the process of interviewing contributors, past data gathered were authenticated and validated. The information pertaining to KM and RM in IT related projects was authenticated through the process of triangulation between the interviewees.

REFERENCES

IRM. (2002). A Risk Management Standard. London: The Institute of Risk Management.

ISO. (2009). *Risk management—Principles and guidelines*. Geneva: ISO.

Jha, N. K. (2008). *Research Methodology*. Chandigarh: Global Media.

Jiang, J. J., Klein, G., Wu, S. P. J., & Liang, T. P. (2008). The relation of requirements uncertainty and stakeholder perception gaps to project management performance. *Journal of Systems and Software, 82*(5), 801-808. doi:10.1016/j.jss.2008.11.833

Jones, H. (2005). Risking knowledge management: An information audit of risk management activities within the Hobart City Council. *Library Management, 26*(6/7), 397-407. doi:10.1108/01435120410609806

Kalling, T., & Styhre, A. (n.d.). *Knowledge Sharing in Organizations*. Malmö. *LiberAB*.

Kleindorfer, P. R. (2011). *Risk management for energy efficiency projects in developing countries*. Vienna: Development Policy, Statistics and Research Branch.

Knight, F. H. (2006). *Risk, Uncertainty and Profit*. New York: Cosimo Inc.

Koskinen, K. U. (2010). Recursive view of the project-based companies' knowledge production. *Journal of Knowledge Management, 14*(2), 258–268. doi:10.1108/13673271011032391

Kothari, C. R. (2004). *Research Methodology: Methods and Techniques*. Delhi: New Age International.

Kutsch, E., & Hall, M. (2010). Deliberate ignorance in project risk management. *International Journal of Project Management, 28*(3), 245-255. doi:10.1016/j.ijproman.2009.05.003

Lai, M.-F., & Lee, G.-G. (2007). Risk-avoiding cultures toward achievement of knowledge sharing. *Business Process Management Journal, 13*(4), 522-537. doi:10.1108/14637150710763559

Leonard-Barton, D. (1995). *Wellsprings of Knowledge: Building and Sustaining the Sources of Innovation*. Cambridge, MA: Harvard Business School Press.

López-Nicolás, C., & Merono-Cerdán, Á. L. (2011). *Strategic knowledge management, innovation and performance. International Journal of Information Management, 31(6)*, 502–509. doi:10.1016/j.ijinfomgt.2011.02.003

Mabudafhasi, R. (2002). The Role of Knowledge Management and Information Sharing in Capacity Building for Sustainable Development. Pretoria: Ocean & Coastal Management. Available at http://www.sciencedirect.com/science/article/pii/S0964569102000947

Massingham, P. (2010). Knowledge risk management: A framework. *Journal of Knowledge Management, 14*(3), 464-485. doi:10.1108/13673271011050166

Maylor, H. (2010). *Project Management* (4th ed.). Essex, UK: Pearson Education Limited.

NASA. (2008). *Knowledge Management*. Available at: http://km.nasa.gov/whatis/index.html

Neef, D. (2005). Managing corporate risk through better knowledge management. *The Learning Organization, 12*(2), 112-124. doi:10.1108/09696470510583502

Nicolini, D., Gherardi, S., & Yanow, D. (2003). *Knowing in Organizations: A Practice-Based Approach*. New York: M.E. Sharpe.

Nonaka, I., & Takeuchi, H. (1995). *The Knowledge-Creating Company: How Japanese Companies Create the Dynamics of Innovation*. New York: Oxford University Press.

O'Donnell, A. M., Dansereau, D. F., & Hall, R. H. (2002). Knowledge Maps as Scaffolds for Cognitive Processing. *Educational Psychology Review, 14*(1), 71–86. doi:10.1023/A:1013132527007

OECD. (2004). *The Significance of Knowledge Management in the Business Sector*. Washington, DC: Public Affairs and Communications Directorate. Available at: http://www.oecd.org/publications/Pol_brief

PMBOK. (2008). *A Guide to the Project Management Body of Knowledge* (4th ed.). Project Management Institute.

Pun, K. F., & Nathai-Balkissoon, M. (2011). Integrating knowledge management into organizational learning: A review of concepts and models. *The Learning Organization, 18*(3), 203-223. doi:10.1108/09696471111123261

Punch, K. F. (2005). *Introduction to Social Research: Quantitative and Qualitative approaches (2nd ed.)*. London: Sage Publications.

Chapter 4
Discussion

ABSTRACT

The chapter offers a thorough deliberation about the available information in the shape of scrutinized data collected by means of primary and secondary sources. The interpretation of findings has been carried out. This is followed by an in-depth analysis. After that, a thorough discussion is made by examining and scrutinizing the objectives of the study.

DOI: 10.4018/978-1-5225-8389-9.ch004

INTERPRETATION OF FINDINGS

PM in the IT department of the several organizations has evolved since the end of the 1990s. At that time, IT projects had an engineering focus, with an emphasis on delivery of projects that performed the tasks as specified in the requirements. The failure rate of IT projects as reported by the Standish Group's *Chaos Report* was 31% of the IT projects (Eve *et al.*,2010). The project process involved a small group of people that were not part of a larger system of the organization. IT projects now involve many people who are working in different locations in the United States. There are also project team members who are not in the United States and who have a major role in the process. The IT project must be integrated into the complex existing IT environment that processes most of the insurance policies for the business. The IT members who will be maintaining the system after the project implementation must know the operations of the project. They are responsible for correcting problems that may occur when the project is part of the operating IT environment for the organization. In the effort to keep all of the stakeholders involved in the IT project, sharing knowledge is critical.

This study analyzed the below mentioned questions:

Findings of RQ1

RQ1: How the tools and techniques of KM is being used in your organization in the design and execution of IT projects?

The PM techniques used a project life-cycle approach of four phases: (a) concept, (b) planning, (c) execution, and (d) termination. The organization followed this approach to IT projects but was moving toward an adaptive approach. There was one group that still used a predictive approach. The adaptive approach still follows the four phases, but the planning and execution phases are performed in a shorter time span than the traditional predictive approach. The research found that different repository KM tools were being used in the life-cycle approach. The different tools aided the team members in the different phases for the success of the project. MS SharePoint and Rally were used in the requirements and analysis process to organize and understand the needs of the users. IBM WebSphere was used by the IT team to design and implement user requirements. During the design process for the project, a design review was used to ensure the inclusion of the quality and best-practices standards of the organization. After completing the design, the coding of the project was performed. HP Quality Center was used in the testing phase to ensure that user requirements were being taken care of in the process of the system.

As per the studies of the authors (Ziolkowski *et al.*,2013), study on KM also broke the systems development process into phases, and their research focused on the requirements phase. Their study suggested that there was a need for clearer definition of the roles and processes of the project team members. Without the clear definition of the roles of team members, there was confusion about the ability of team members to perform tasks and apply knowledge to the project. With this insurance organization, the project team did not seem to have this issue. The team members seemed to have been able to work with each other to find the knowledge needed for the project.

The PMBOK® includes ten knowledge areas: (i) "integration management", (ii) "scope management", (iii) "time management", (iv) "cost management", (v) "quality management", (vi) "human resources management", (vii) "communications management", (viii) "risk management", (ix) "procurement management", and (x) "stakeholder management" (PMI,2013). These 10 knowledge areas were part of the PM process at all the organization whose IT professional have been interviewed during the course of research work.. Scope management, time management, procurement management and risk management, used MS SharePoint or Rally in the different projects in the requirements process of the project. Quality management and integration management were part of the HP Quality Center and the testing process. Stakeholder management and communication management were done with the face-to-face tools and stored in MS SharePoint during the development of the project. By the process of the project areas and permitting the individuals of the IT area, the human resources management for the projects was performed. The management of the projects performed cost management throughout the PM process.

KM research is frequently focused on the knowledge acquisition encompassed by KM processes, sharing of knowledge, and knowledge creation (Stirbu *et al.*,2014). In this research, the KM process was associated with the PM phases. In their research on business process and KM, the authors (Cao *et al.*,2013) have examined the task-technology fit in three global technology firms. The research found a relationship between the business process and the KM technology in a similar manner that the research on IT PM did. For this research on IT PM, the business processes were requirements gathering, code development, testing the system, and helpdesk processes. The research identified the technology involving KM tools and techniques for the different processes.

Findings of RQ2

RQ2: How can you justify that the KM tools and techniques used in organization for IT PM increase the success of an IT project.

The findings of the second research question focused on the success of the IT project. The IT area of the organization placed a priority on the highest quality software that could be developed. The lack of defects that occurred with the software when placed in production was the indication of success. The lower the number of defects, the higher the rate of success would be for the project. The goal was for zero defects for a project, but that was not usually obtained. For high-quality systems, the organization had design and code reviews. The testing phase was a three-step process to discover all defects with the project and correct them before being placed in production.

Fewer defects in the software caused the user to have a advanced degree of satisfaction with the project. These standards impacted a knowledge sharing that occurred in the project and after the project was implemented. In (Olson *et al.*,2013), the authors have studied the use of KM in quality management for products. Their results indicated that the application of KM techniques for sharing tacit and explicit knowledge had a positive impact on the quality of products. In (Wang *et al.*,2014), the authors also studied the connection between quality management and KM systems and found the same results as the authors of (Ghandwar *et al.*,2013) studied KM and quality management in the insurance industry and also found relationship between KM and quality management.

The findings of the second research question also include the different tools and techniques used for KM. MS SharePoint was used as a repository for the project. This repository contained the documents for the project, including scope, requirements, and testing information. MS SharePoint was also used as a knowledge-sharing tool, with discussion boards for exchanging ideas about the project. Documents added to MS SharePoint also included information about the individual who added the document to the repository. This information created a knowledge map for the user of SharePoint to find an expert on the subject. For the business areas that used an adaptive approach, in addition to MS SharePoint, Rally was used to share user stories about the processes of the project. A KM system was developed using MS Access as the primary repository tool. The MS Access system contained user rules and procedures needed for the development of new applications. E-mail, video conferencing, and instant messaging were used to share face-to-face knowledge. These tools were different from the tools referred to by the authors, which include Gantt charts, work breakdown structure, and flow charts. They were also different from the mind maps and concept maps referred to by the authors (Wang *et al.*,2011). Instead of using the specific tools as discussed by (Patanakul *et al.*,2010), the organization used Rally and MS SharePoint, which incorporated those tools. By incorporating the specific tools in other products, the team members were able to use one product and share knowledge for the project.

The organization used KM repository and face-to-face tools for timely access to the knowledge needed for the project. The face-to-face tools such as instant messaging and e-mail were used to gather the tacit knowledge for the project. The respondents referred in the process of codification, the data then needed to be converted to explicit knowledge and stored in a data repository such as MS SharePoint, Rally, or Remedy. In the PM process, without these KM tools, finding the right knowledge at the right time was a challenge. The current tools were not always effective for the project, but they were better than the past process with file sharing, paper, and telephone calls. By identifying the processes for the knowledge and where the issues are, the organization could work to correct them for more successful projects.

The respondents suggested that a process-oriented culture improved knowledge sharing. This seemed to be the case for the project teams at the insurance team. There was a concern for sharing knowledge in each phase to improve the process. The focus was not always results-oriented, but the process of the different models being performed as well as possible. The project teams focused on the success of the project and the highest quality possible, but in each of the phases attention was paid to sharing knowledge for that process.

Findings of RQ3

RQ3: How is the current PM process managing knowledge for an IT project?

The findings of the research on the current PM process for managing knowledge answered the third research question. To improve the knowledge of standards some changes in the process such as senior IT people conducting code reviews and a separate group of the IT area reviewing the design of new systems have been implemented. These changes have improved the knowledge sharing for the projects. It has helped all team members understand design standards and the best practices for the organization.

This knowledge had been missing in the past, and by improving the knowledge flow, the number of defects that the production area encountered has fallen. The process of having IT team members of completed projects available for new projects accomplished the objective of having team members' work with new teams and sharing their knowledge. The problem was the team members started realizing they wanted to stay with the same team members. They had developed a working relationship with these team members and did not want to disrupt this. The IT area moved to a structure with the project areas, and the team members did not move to new areas as they did in the past. This change helped the knowledge transfer because team members had worked with the others before. The relationships between team members were maintained and helped the team develop quality projects. As one manager described it, And what we found is, once you form a project team, and you build those and you build that cadence, and you build that, "Well, here's what I'm good at. Here's what you're good at," that if we keep that project team together longer, we begin to build velocity that we couldn't get in the other model that we had.

This process created an autopoietic system for the team members . By keeping the team together, the world created by the knowledge of the group was built on for the next IT project. This world used an understandable language for the team members, as suggested by. With an understandable language and an increased level of trust, knowledge sharing for the team rose. This team structure increased the knowledge sharing because it followed the four criteria of: (a) To know what the other person knows, (b) admission to that very person in a timely manner, (c) one person is willing to help the other, and (d) an extent of safety. Trust in the relationship as identified by the authors of for their study of knowledge sharing also rose. The respondents suggested that the strong tacit knowledge sharing that had occurred in the project team gave the project team a flexibility to work with different team members. This made it possible for the different members of the IT business area to work with different team members from the same business area for successful projects. This process also created as a place where knowledge was shared, created, and utilized. In this process, the team members were moved closer together, and the ability to meet was enhanced. There were also conference rooms for each project to share project knowledge.

Findings of RQ4

RQ4: How does the PKM model for managing knowledge improve the success of an IT project?

The findings of the last research question examined PKM to improve the success of the project. The model was applied differently for the different processes of the project and used different repositories. The requirements process involved knowledge sharing between the business area and the IT groups with MS SharePoint and Rally. The design review that is part of the code development includes other projects. Reliant on the scope and size of a project, it could also comprise other departments. For the testing process, the knowledge sharing was between the quality assurance area and the IT groups, with HP Quality Center as the repository. The code development process focused on the individuals of the IT area and their knowledge to develop the code for the project, with IBM WebSphere as the repository. The helpdesk processing involved knowledge sharing between the users and the IT area, with Remedy as the repository. The users included both employees inside the organization and external clients who used the systems to perform business. Knowledge was also acquired from external sources, which included different courses that are available, outside consultants, the Internet, and user groups. The knowledge that was acquired using the different techniques based on the process that the knowledge needed.

The PKM models used five types of knowledge transfer of (a) between persons, (b) between individuals and external structures, (c) between individuals and internal structures, (d) between external arrangements or structures and individuals, and (e) inside the internal arrangement or structure. The IT area had incorporated these five types of knowledge transfer. As the project teams moved to an adaptive process, there was more emphasis placed on the IT project teams and the users for the requirements processing. Team members needed to learn the adaptive process. A training course that occurred at another facility of the organization provided this. For external knowledge acquisition, the organization also brought in external consultants to provide knowledge about the adaptive processing. IT team members were involved in external organizations and conferences to add knowledge. One of the important parts of the design and code reviews was the knowledge transfer between the individuals and the internal structures of the IT area. During these reviews, best practices and design standards for the organization were shared among project teams. The design and code reviews included the platform support area for involving the production area with the project teams in the IT area.

The organizations whose professionals have participated in the study did not have many of opportunities for the team members to add external knowledge to the firm by attending external courses and conferences. The process for gathering knowledge was focused within the organization. This could be a concern as discussed with the respondents in a study on the importance of external sources of knowledge for use in the strategic decisions of the organization. Their analysis indicated that as an organization increased the use of external knowledge there was an increase in the ability of the organization to exploit new opportunities. This research showed the importance of external knowledge and the need for an organization to use it for a strategic advantage.

Findings of RQ5

RQ5: To what extent, in your esteemed organization, the KM practices are developed or mature?

The findings of this research question depict that most of the respondents candidly and truthfully said that in their organization the KM practices are in their infancy stage. The major contributing factor to this "ignorance" is that the people deployed on different projects in different capacities have perception that the sharing of knowledge does not guarantee any benefits in the form of bonuses and / or promotion. Furthermore, by throwing this question to the interviewees, the author came to know that the high echelon of the organizations does not know about the emerging field of KM. Also, as the executives of the organization are ignorant about KM, they even on the proposals or requests of the employees are not convinced to arrange training session(s) on KM for their employees.

Findings of RQ6

RQ6: In what manner would you describe the application or utilization of KM in your esteemed organization?

The findings of this research question depict that KM is not formally utilized in the organizations which are contributing for this research work. The respondents told the author that in their organizations either the practices of KM are not being practiced or practiced not under the name of KM.

Findings of RQ7

RQ7: Do your organization has any documented policy as far KM tools & techniques are concerned?

The findings of this research question depict that as in most of the organizations the KM is in infancy there is formal or approved documented policy is available. Employees on their own will and wish share their acquired knowledge or gained experience with their co-workers, consciously or unconsciously.

Findings of RQ8

RQ8: At what extent your organization practices the tools, techniques or methods (Storytelling, Benchmarking, Brainstorming etc.) for KM?

The findings of this research question depict that as there is no formal policy available on KM in the organizations whose IT professionals have been interviewed, the large number of respondents said that unconsciously the method Storytelling and Brainstorming are being the by employees. This unconscious practice of KM methods do not guarantee the success of an IT project, and according to the respondents no big breakthrough in the success rate of IT projects has been witnessed yet.

Findings of RQ9

RQ9: At what extent your organization practices the tools, techniques or methods (SWOT, PESTEL, FMEA etc.) for RM?

The findings of this research question reveal that SWOT and PESTEL techniques are being utilized upto a very high level of magnitude. The respondents reveals the primary reason of their usage that these methods were formally taught at university level. Also, their respective organizations also arrange the trainings sessions on regular basis to fresh the concepts of these methods.

Findings of RQ10

RQ10: To what extent the sources of risk (like information unavailability, inappropriate flow of information etc.) affect your esteemed organization?

The respondents reveal that the sources of risks like information unavailability, inappropriate flow of information etc. have greatly affected the flow of projects in the past which brought bad names to the organizations. The respondents urged that if the KM practices are formally accepted and practiced in their organizations the success ratio of IT would fall down exponentially and that might lead to bankruptcy.

Findings of RQ11

RRQ11: In your viewpoint how the techniques and approaches of KM & RM share similarities?

Almost all of the respondents are of the opinion that the techniques and approaches of KM & RM share similarities in that they both emphasis on apprehending, obtaining and generating knowledge and information.

Findings of RQ12

RQ12: In your perspective, is there any scope available for incorporating KM tool & techniques into RM tool & techniques?

In answer to that question in fact all the respondents were of the view that right from the beginning of the project both the workers and management must be in line as far as KM and RM techniques are concerned.

Findings of RQ13

RQ13: Would you like to give any suggestions / recommendations for KM and RM as well as for joint functioning?

The respondents replied this question both from the structural and technological standpoints. Both the viewpoints will be discussed thoroughly in the subsequent paragraphs.

KM Tools for Different Project Stages

This section scrutinizes the risk areas of this research and assesses which of the KM techniques as described in the literature review can be made practical to invalidate or lower the influence of identified risks. In the process of doing it, it depends on the literature review and a large amount of information has been obtained from reading various articles and books (which was a part stretched literature review. The comprehensive literature review delivered the in-depth approaches as well as methodology to make them practical. This is basically the broad shape of the ideas and concepts previously told in the literature review. They are delivered with credit to the identical sources but additional information was added. The inclusion and in-depth analysis of learning, feedback and Suggestions, that belong to the primary data was also carried.

Information Non Availability

This can be termed as an acute source of a risk and can be handled by applying the suitable KM tools and techniques. The arrangement and organization of "Brain Storming Session" is the first and foremost requirement. This approach will be beneficial not only for the project team but also to the organization in its entirety as it helps the project team members by thinking upon the challenging state or situation while keeping the minds away from the hustle and bustle of normal working stress (Maylor *et al.*,2010). This thing plays a role of a medium which shares the "Best Practices" prevails in different project teams of the organizations and hence leads to amalgamation of the "*Lessons Learnt*" into existing strategies via the apprehending and using of "*Past Experiences*" *(Farias et al..,2003).* This is built on the concept of 'Case-Based reasoning" that relates the fresh problem with a preceding like situation and practices the knowledge and information belongs to that particular situation producing the solution based on it.

Beside this, the information has a flexibility which enables it to get congregated by using "Cross-Project" (Artto *et al.,*2000). It is desirable that the learning through individuals must be transferred and not just the knowledge. As it is established during the interviews sessions, in this very manner new ideas and thoughts erupt which might have been missing because of "*aligned* thinking" of the members of project team. This is able to contribute in the use of knowledge database of the organization (knowledge repositories in the form of reports, files, and several other form of documents) which has been shaped for this very purpose and result in "*Leveraging the Intellectual Assets*" in the form of "*Knowledge Maps*". These KM tools are briefed in Figure 1.

Absence of a Mutually Defined Context

It is a well-defined fact that the Organizations need four interacting features or elements which include people, task, technology and structure that necessitate

Figure 1. KM tools available for information non availability

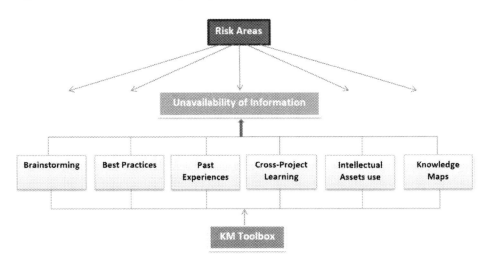

combined effect among these elements (Boddy *et al.*,2002). At this time due to the fact the organizational structure is different from the project, the individuals and task are considered as the most significant elements but portray self-styled organizations. With the aid of present organizational context and by virtue of informal and formal communications hence a social context is developed which helps in achieving different objectives of the project, in this way the project is started (Zhang *et al.*,2010). Because of this reason, the *"Embedding of knowledge"* in services, products and processes of a project turn out to be necessary.

As it has been proposed during the interviews sessions, the primary task is to bring into line the entire project team and all the project stakeholders for the formation of shared context. This encompasses the general understanding of various terms of project like scope (exclusion & inclusion), aim, purpose, goals and objectives constraints and deliverables but the most important is the assumptions upon which the total estimates are developed (Zhang *et al.*,2010). It has now become relevant to examine the assumption and decisions taken by the project manager there forth. This can be completed by virtue of *"Knowledge fairs"* (for the involvement of stakeholder) that shapes the *"Best Practices"* of project. The *"Workshops* stage", the" *Brainstorming sessions"* execution for the purpose of comprehension of goals and challenges of a project to formulate the project goals and objectives that are "SMART (Specific, Measurable, Achievable, Realistic, Time oriented)" and acceptable to all. This concluding step is the acceptance and description of the process and procedure belong to the change management in order to impose it. The available tools required for the accomplishment of this purpose are briefed in Figure 2.

Inadequate Information Flow

This concerns to the information flow amongst the different stakeholders of the project by virtue of "knowledge spiral". In order to manage this type of a risk is to instill the duty for *"Knowledge Sharing"*. This could be achieved by virtue of motivation that can be executed by using the incentives like *"Rewards"*. This possesses the purpose of comprehending and measuring the worth of knowledge. Based on the studies completed by the authors (Lai *et al.*,2007) have established that a well-structured "empowerment system" cares and delivers a solid base for KM guiding towards unparalleled trust that has inclinations headed for the knowledge sharing . Furthermore, the

Figure 2. KM tools for absence of defined context

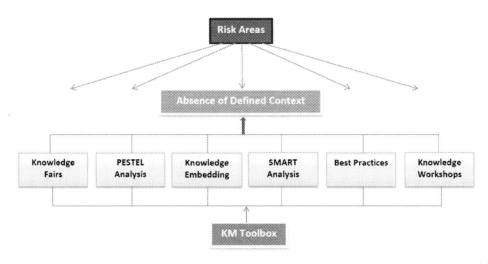

other method that has got recognition is the method of *"After Action reviews"* that is applied for the creation of *"Best Practices"* made upon the *"Lessons Learnt"* in earlier projects hence offering the inertia for steering the project in the lack of adequate information.

In order to ensure the suitable floe of knowledge, there is a requirement for the development "Knowledge Database" or "Repositories" that can be accessed as and when required. They all are termed as "formal approaches" being used to preserve the sources of knowledge. As it has been revealed during the interview sessions, the formation of "Communities of Practice" (COP's) is the one of the most effective and fruitful methodologies for sharing of knowledge. This very concept supports in the process of information sharing through *"Storytelling"* that aids in shifting "tacit knowledge". As elaborated in the literature review, the formal "Knowledge Map" can be made structured with this informal that play a vital. All these valid tools are briefed in Figure 3.

Lack of Common Framework of Reference

It is a common practice that different departments within the same organization use different methods for the management of risks. The down side of this approach is that it induces the evils of poor collaboration and incompatibility

Figure 3. KM tools for insufficient flow of information

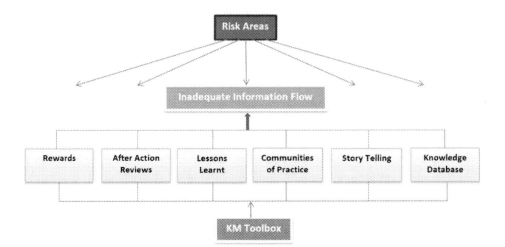

as far as the knowledge base is concerned. But to make the project success it is considered vital to abide by that the strategies adopted for managing risks must be same throughout the project (Farias *et al.*,2003). "Benchmarking", that is a technique of KM has the potential to work effectively in this condition or situation. This can be achieved by practicing *"Knowledge Audit"* during the course of the project. This method is considered as the most fruitful method for handling the risks and hence can be proposed to all the departments to pursue, in that way it will lead to a same framework that can be utilized by all the departments to increase and alter the heading of action. In this way both the quantitative and qualitative tools of RM can be incorporated, so that on a common agreement and evaluation of risks can be developed.

The "Knowledge Maps", which is a KM tool, after establishment can identify the major knowledge areas, resources, in-house expertise etc. This paves the way for the enrichment of risk planning skills of the managers having experience and knowledge (Farias *et al.*,2003). As it is revealed in primary research, this is to be united with benchmarking (internally inside the project and externally with the business) guides to the establishment of newest methods that are extra effective in handling the risks in a much improved way. The valid tools that can be used for this purpose are briefed in Figure 4.

Figure 4. KM tools for lack of framework of reference

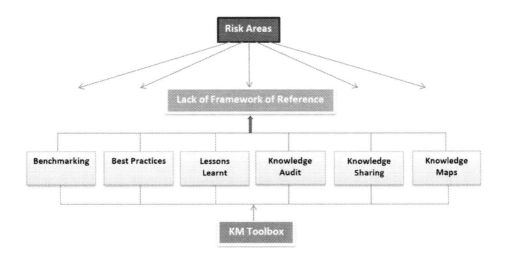

Ineffective Linkage Systems

In order to augment the value and worth of the knowledge and information related to a project must be connected together. The establishment of "KM Maps", which links the sources of knowledge together is considered as the best KM technique. The sources of knowledge n "Knowledge Maps" are connected through node-links in which the information is stored or located in nodes and the connected links are labelled. By virtue of "Knowledge Audit" the node-links will be revealed". As for the sake of external knowledge, the knowledge centers or bases have become essential for the purpose of customer building and mining.

That helps in "Embedding the information and knowledge" as far as the processes, services and products of projects are concerned. Other supportive KM techniques comprise the concept of assigning titles such as "*Knowledge workers, CKOs* (Chief Knowledge Officers), *Knowledge brokers* (persons acting as a reference for information on explicit topics, subjects or fields) and many others.

These structures in relation to ICT systems are a compulsory media for the management of risk knowledge associated with the project despite they are not enough in themselves without the intervention of human interface or human interaction. The systems of such nature answer the reason of connecting the knowledge areas by utilizing "*Collaborative Technologies* (groupware, etc.)", as a "*Social Software*" and many others. As the technology is advancing, few authors encouraging the utilization of framework that appreciates the computerization or automation of few main stages of RM connected to the process of decision making hence guiding the risk response planning modest, accurate and even more faster (Lunaardi *et al.*,2012). It is established on the notion of utilizing the available historical knowledge (information available from earlier projects) and centering the decisions on the basis of it by connecting and discovering the commonalities between the present and the earlier risks and also the relevant methodologies utilized to handle them. If implemented appropriately this can turn out to be beneficial. This can prove advantageous if applied properly. The entire range of valid tools for this very purpose are briefed in Figure 5.

Rapid Change in Technology

This type of risk that associated with the planning and execution of the IT projects that can be mitigated by applying the certain KM tools and

Figure 5. KM tools for ineffective linkage systems

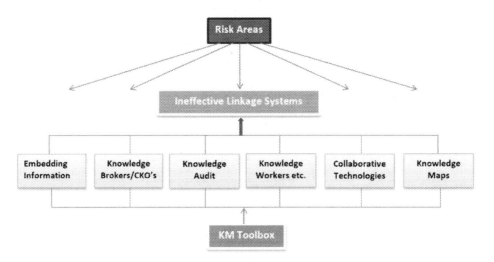

techniques. The first and foremost techniques is to employ the technique of "Brainstorming". During the planning phase of the project, the financial aspect must be taken in account at a deeper level. All the personnel involved in the planning of the must share their views openly with their project team members. So that they reach to certain level of making a financial decision.

Secondly, the "Best Practices" approach is to be utilized. The project team members who have a finance background must be fully conversant with all the best practices in vogue in different organizations of the world.

Another approach is to share the "Past Experiences" related to technological turmoil / incidents the project team members have experienced during their professional carrier. A thorough deliberation is required to be made and that deliberation may lead to the formulation of financial standards and procedures of the organization.

"Knowledge Audit" is another technique that can be utilized to mitigate the technology risks. Before, during and after the completion of the project, the project team members must sit together to review the constraints they have faced in the recently completed IT project and based on those experiences they have to review the current or prevailing financial standards and modify them accordingly to prevent the problems in the future IT projects.

The organization can also take the advantage of the intellectuals available at their disposal who have sufficient background in the domain of finance or financial risk management. The judicious utilization of "Intellectual Assets" guarantees the minimization of financial constraints in the future IT project.

The financial constraints can further be minimized by assigning the responsibilities to the project team member(s) of "Knowledge Workers", "Chief Knowledge Officers", "Knowledge Brokers" etc.

Financial Constraints

This type of risk that is inherently associated with the planning and execution of the IT projects that can be mitigated by applying the certain KM tools and techniques. The first and foremost techniques is to employ the technique of "Brainstorming". During the planning phase of the project, the financial aspect must be taken in account at a deeper level. All the personnel involved in the planning of the must share their views openly with their project team members. So that they reach to certain level of making a financial decision.

Figure 6. KM tools for rapid change in technology

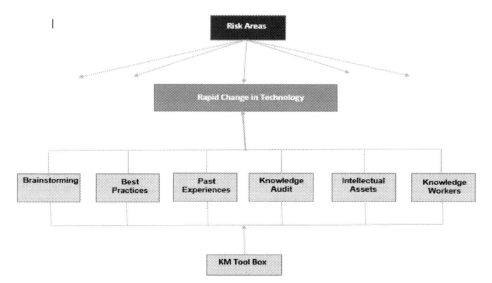

Secondly, the "Best Practices" approach is to be utilized. The project team members who have a finance background must be fully conversant with all the best practices in vogue in different organizations of the world.

Another approach is to share the "Past Experiences" related to financial turmoil / incidents the project team members have experienced during their professional carrier. A thorough deliberation is required to be made and that deliberation may lead to the formulation of financial standards and procedures of the organization.

"Knowledge Audit" is another technique that can be utilized to mitigate the financial risks. Before, during and after the completion of the project, the project team members must sit together to review the constraints they have faced in the recently completed IT project and based on those experiences they have to review the current or prevailing financial standards and modify them accordingly to prevent the problems in the future IT projects.

The organization can also take the advantage of the intellectuals available at their disposal who have sufficient background in the domain of finance or financial risk management. The judicious utilization of "Intellectual Assets" guarantees the minimization of financial constraints in the future IT project.

Figure 7. KM tools for financial constraints

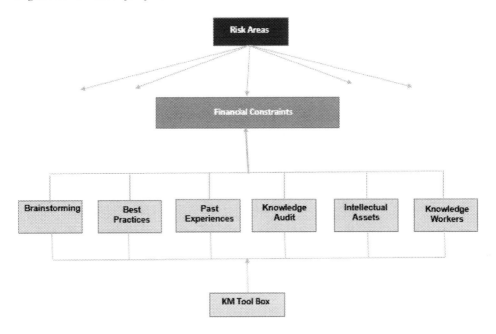

The financial constraints can further be minimized by assigning the responsibilities to the project team member(s) of "Knowledge Workers", "Chief Knowledge Officers", "Knowledge Brokers" etc.

Security Risks

This type of risk that is inherently associated with the planning and execution of the IT projects that can be mitigated by applying the certain KM tools and techniques. The first and foremost techniques is to employ the technique of "Brainstorming". During the planning phase of the project, the financial aspect must be taken in account at a deeper level. All the personnel involved in the planning of the must share their views openly with their project team members. So that they reach to certain level of making a financial decision.

Secondly, the "Best Practices" approach is to be utilized. The project team members who have a Security background must be fully conversant with all the best practices in vogue in different organizations of the world.

Another approach is to share the "Past Experiences" related to security turmoil / incidents the project team members have experienced during their professional carrier. A thorough deliberation is required to be made and that deliberation may lead to the formulation of financial standards and procedures of the organization.

"Knowledge Audit" is another technique that can be utilized to mitigate such risks. Before, during and after the completion of the project, the project team members must sit together to review the constraints they have faced in the recently completed IT project and based on those experiences they have to review the current or prevailing financial standards and modify them accordingly to prevent the problems in the future IT projects.

The organization can also take the advantage of the intellectuals available at their disposal who have sufficient background in the domain of finance or financial risk management. The judicious utilization of "Intellectual Assets" guarantees the minimization of financial constraints in the future IT project.

The financial constraints can further be minimized by assigning the responsibilities to the project team member(s) of "Knowledge Workers", "Chief Knowledge Officers", "Knowledge Brokers" etc.

Figure 8. KM tools for security risks

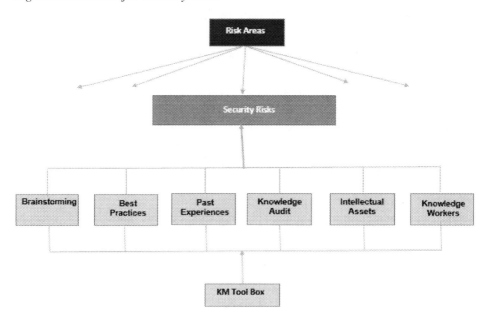

Risks Associated With Human Resources

This type of risk that is inherently associated with the planning and execution of the IT projects that can be mitigated by applying the certain KM tools and techniques. The first and foremost techniques is to employ the technique of "Brainstorming". During the planning phase of the project, the financial aspect must be taken in account at a deeper level. All the personnel involved in the planning of the must share their views openly with their project team members. So that they reach to certain level of making a correct decision.

Secondly, the "Best Practices" approach is to be utilized. The project team members who have a HR background must be fully conversant with all the best practices in vogue in different organizations of the world.

Another approach is to share the "Past Experiences" related to employee turnover the project team members have experienced during their professional carrier. A thorough deliberation is required to be made and that deliberation may lead to the formulation of financial standards and procedures of the organization.

"Knowledge Audit" is another technique that can be utilized to mitigate the HR risks. Before, during and after the completion of the project, the project team members must sit together to review the constraints they have faced in the recently completed IT project and based on those experiences they have to review the current or prevailing financial standards and modify them accordingly to prevent the problems in the future IT projects.

The organization can also take the advantage of the intellectuals available at their disposal who have sufficient background in the domain of HR management. The judicious utilization of "Intellectual Assets" guarantees the minimization of financial constraints in the future IT project.

The HR constraints can further be minimized by assigning the responsibilities to the project team member(s) of "Knowledge Workers", "Chief Knowledge Officers", "Knowledge Brokers" etc.

Risks of Success

This type of risk that is inherently associated with the planning and execution of the IT projects that can be mitigated by applying the certain KM tools and techniques. The first and foremost techniques is to employ the technique

Figure 9. Risks associated with human resources

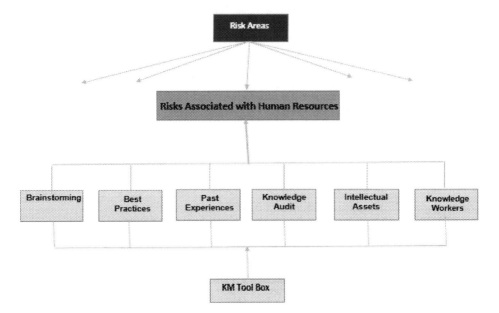

of "Brainstorming". During the planning phase of the project, the success aspect must be taken in account at a deeper level. All the personnel involved in the planning of the must share their views openly with their project team members. So that they reach to certain level of making a correct decision.

Secondly, the "Best Practices" approach is to be utilized. The project team members who have a RM background must be fully conversant with all the best practices in vogue in different organizations of the world.

Another approach is to share the "Past Experiences" related to Success Risks the project team members have experienced during their professional carrier. A thorough deliberation is required to be made and that deliberation may lead to the formulation of pertinent standards and procedures of the organization.

"Knowledge Audit" is another technique that can be utilized to mitigate the success risks. Before, during and after the completion of the project, the project team members must sit together to review the constraints they have faced in the recently completed IT project and based on those experiences they have to review the current or prevailing standards and modify them accordingly to prevent the problems in the future IT projects.

Figure 10. KM tools for success risks

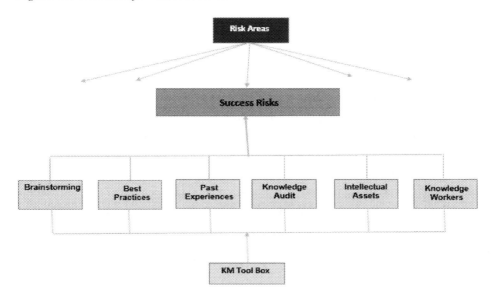

The organization can also take the advantage of the intellectuals available at their disposal who have sufficient background in the domain of risk management. The judicious utilization of "Intellectual Assets" guarantees the minimization of financial constraints in the future IT project.

The financial constraints can further be minimized by assigning the responsibilities to the project team member(s) of "Knowledge Workers", "Chief Knowledge Officers", "Knowledge Brokers" etc.

Commonalities Between KM and RM

For far we have discussed and analyzed the threating sources of risk that have the potential to disturb the execution of risk in any part or stage of the project keeping in view the utilization of KM tools and techniques, Now, the current discussion moves to the subsequent stage where the commonalties between the approaches of KM and RM are scrutinized. The extended literature review of M tools and techniques which was undertaken in the earlier part of this research will be utilized in this section and learning from previous section which has embedded the recommendations from the conducted interviews. The numerous factors and categories of commonalities have been examined and are elaborated below with the explanation and description:

Accumulation of Knowledge

The core aim of KM is to grasp information and convert it into operational knowledge that can be implemented and made it practical. Its drive is to endure and cultivate the organizational capabilities by apprehending the tacit and explicit facets of knowledge (APM 2006). KM resolves the purpose of acquirement of knowledge by discovering present knowledge, comprehending necessities and penetrating through numerous sources. RM resolves the similar purpose but below the perspective of risks. All the cited obstinacies of KM are also untied by RM using comparable tools of brainstorming and other techniques. The discussion that carried out during the meetings is considered as one important parts of RM (PMBOK 2013).

Dissemination of Knowledge

It is the utmost desire of KM efficiently distribute knowledge both in terms of space and time from one corner to other corner of the organization as well as all the project stakeholders. In the shape of the "Risk Register", RM offers equivalent supplies for the purpose of communication, documentation and analysis (PMBOK 2013). The distribution handles the spreading of present information through the translation of data into information and eventually for knowledge sharing (APM 2006). Since both KM and RM are encountering uncertainty (Emblemm *et al.*,2010), control and performance monitoring and emphasis on attaining competitive gain(Zhang *et al.*,2010) . They both (KM and RM) strive to provide systems, processes and infrastructure to back events and activities as well as in the making of decisions (Neef *et al.*,2005) to support knowledge dissemination with upto-date concept of real time evaluations (Arrow *et al.*,2008). Furthermore, RM preserves the lessons learnt for future requirements (PMBOK 2013) a concept formed by KM.

Reprocessing of Knowledge

KM reutilizes knowledge by repetitively using the produced knowledge, which developed at different locations and times. This includes implementing or applying present knowledge for an original purpose as endorsed by the conducted primary research. For the purpose of data and information collection and interpretation the techniques of both KM and RM are used(Jones, 2005).

The techniques of both KM and RM are used for the forming and managing the knowledge(Jones, 2005).These techniques can also be utilized for the purpose of decision making by integrating and utilizing the existing knowledge, (Jones, 2005)..

The knowledge utilized may come from a preceding context but by virtue of a fresh application fresh knowledge is produced. The KM and RM techniques emphasis on the quality and management of information and discards inappropriate information to escape from heaps of irrelevant material] (Jones, 2005).In collaboration, both KM and RM, strive to recognize the experience of users and portray it in black and white the possibilities and analyzed them to sidestep creation of gaps that directs to imperfect decision.

Collaboration

This relates to the alliance at the human as well as the technological level. One of the objectives of KM is to initiate the sense of efficient and effective association among the individuals of project groups and as well as from corner to corner of the entire range of distinct groups. Identical is the state where the RM processes operate together besides other knowledge areas (PMBOK 2013). Both KM and RM examined the existing processes for the identification of gaps and bring into line with the strategic project objectives (PMBOK 2013). Such processes act together and coincides with other processes of PM. The notion of stakeholders along with their analysis and appropriate interaction between them by means of strong channels is grasped and demanded by KM as well as RM (Arrow *et al.*, 2013).

Problems Encountered

There exists some commonalities as far as the encountering of problems are concerned. The main categories examined by the research are discussed below:

1. **Obsolescence:** It is a fact the information being dealt by both turn out to be obsolete as early as it is produced. Keeping in view this down side of both KM and RM domains, timely reach of this varying information to the suitable user has become an issue.
2. **Overloading:** There exists a plethora of information which is collected and a huge chunk of this collected information is inappropriate which

demands deletion to ignore overload. This then makes it hard to obtain valuable and suitable information for practice.

3. **Technology:** Both KM and RM domains experience the controlled applications as far as the technological perspective is concerned. Technology behaves as an integral tool but the entire stress cannot be rested on it. Unnecessary dependence on technology can be lethal as it is mere a enabler of the purpose not it's central part or core.

Integration of KM and RM

The final section of this chapter discovers and investigates the ways for ensuring the incorporation of KM approaches to the ones being utilized by RM. This can be achieved by examining the RM tools and techniques utilized and as well as the approaches and strategies of KM. For that very matter, the commonalities revealed in the preceding section and the information obtained from the conducted interviews are applied. The presented discussion here is communicated by means of four standpoints namely: the perspective of people, the standpoint of structure, the outlook of context and finally the technological viewpoint and provide expressive measures to boost the alliance of KM and RM and their efficacy as well as effectiveness.

The Perspective of People

As per the recommendations of primary research the first and foremost target at the level of project commencement must be to prompt the sense of joint and aligned vision amongst the project leaders and management to increase steady support from all the levels. This supports in the identification of the foremost requirements of the project stakeholders', leading anticipations and their probable impact which can afterwards be bring into line with the objectives of the project. After that the information requires to be transferred to anticipate and mitigate fears to device solutions that is pertinent to every individual of the project team. Also it supports in handling the conceivable partiality because of cultural dissimilarities ascending due to functioning in diverse contexts (PMBOK 2013).

One of the contributing reasons for low knowledge sharing has been due to the notorious subject of "reward systems'. This exists because of the well-known fact that the individual possesses the knowledge is remunerated and recognized instead of the individual who shares it, speaking stress on the individual knowledge instead of the collective knowledge. "Knowledge Mapping" specifies the knowledge gaps when these holders of knowledge withdrawn from the projects. Hence suitable compensation schemes can produce an environment in which information can be shared whole heartedly by collaborative efforts of the members of the project team and where such efforts of knowledge sharing can be cheered and compensated.

To augment efficiency, Knowledge recognition and distribution ought to be in all directions 'Vertical as well as horizontal' at "the project as well as the organizational level". Preferably, this must be a two-way progression which includes both input donated as well as information retrieved. However the culture of managing and sharing information does not operate in separation, therefore it imposes such supporting systems besides policies which assist and improve it.

The ongoing global collective research endeavors at WHO has recognized numerous "push factors" which endorse to provide a custom-made approach to target stakeholders, trustworthy representatives of information, "pull factors" which offers right to use the searchable databases by means of up-to-date information technology and exchange activities to shape and keep relations. This makes the problem solving environment and encourages the optimal planning heading to the application of fruitful RM solutions. For that vey matter, the use of concepts such as "*Peer Network* for knowledge sharing" where new employees deliberate and learn through experienced peers can be valuable. This can operate in parallel with "COP's" both at intra and inter project levels and encourages the use social networks for casual sharing of experiences. Lastly, collaboration with outside partners or consultants for "*Benchmarking*" *can* also support in the contrast of RM practices that can be applied for "*Gap Analysis*" to attain suitable "knowledge mapping". The perception of KM and RM integration from this viewpoint is shortened in Figure 11.

The Context Outlook

As it has been established that the project offers foundation for learning, the exchange of information must be prompted at the most basic stage that requires a mutual context. KM by means of sharing of knowledge can enable a platform for exchange of ideas in the form of an organizational context that is detained by unrecognizability and exclusiveness (Boddy *et al.*, 2002) to handle

Figure 11. Concept for integrating KM into RM: The people's perspective

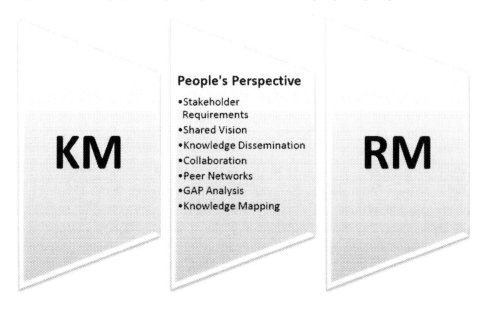

the risks. The context is a key concern as it impacts the communications of individuals and is itself inclined towards the individuals that can support RM.

As context outlook obliges both inside and outside situations of the organization, any disparity in it can make dealing of the project thought-provoking that may assist or impede the comprehension of its purposes, deliverables and advantages. Hence the context has to anticipate the criticality and comprehension of the issue and effect all stakeholders upon which it is founded (APM 2006). This problem of RM can be assisted by means of the suitable tools of KM. Though the far-reaching dispersion of knowledge demands it to be of context-free in nature, it once more time ought to be reinterpreted by means of KM approaches to shape it explicit to the context in order to apply it to match specific conditions (Patton *et al.*,2012) of RM. As it is provided by the interview sessions, "Kick Off meetings" for the purpose of ice breaking, as chunk of the KM procedure, with internal stakeholders, project teams, outer consultants, and many others with the consequence of seeing them as strategic partners be able to solve this issue. For the sake of their optimal alliance, as supported by the primary research, RM must be initiated at project level and KM must be initiated at the organizational level along with SWOT analysis at all the stages of the project. The perception of KM and RM integration from this viewpoint is shortened in Figure 12.

Figure 12. Concept for integrating KM into RM: The context outlook

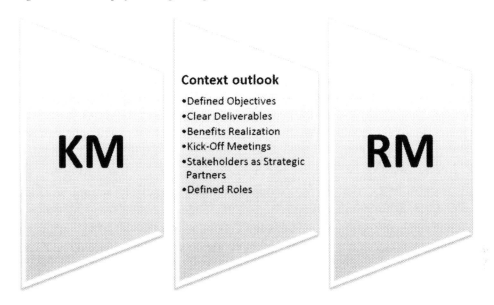

The Structural Viewpoint

This relates to the organizational frameworks and structures at a position for supporting the KM and RM processes that required to be supportive for the sharing of knowledge. A combined project framework increases the extent of standardization which outlines and creates the project deliverables, roles, procedures and responsibilities abundantly clear (Klein *et al.*, 2011) and creates the risk areas obvious to handle them. The intentions of RM can be achieved effortlessly if this framework is incorporated. This incorporation aids in the recognition of novel frameworks. This can be achieved by the establishment of "project office". The "Project Office" as portion of organizational structure provides help and care to stakeholders and clients, comprising consultation sessions, briefings, workshops and presentations.

The paper published by "United Nations Industrial Development Organization" encompassing RM in one of their projects that recommends that maximum number of issues get up at the "identification stage and can be fixed and lessened by enhancing the level of information while applying better steady approaches to project RM . This will be achieved if RM is applied at project level and KM at organizational level with the optimal cooperation besides the project procedures that are compliant reliant on the complexity and size of the project.

The "World Bank Group" task managers endeavor to achieve valid and methodical ways to apply information management practices to alleviate risks by means of the mechanisms of culpability and stiffening control(Edwards *et al.*,2009). This can be developed capable by means of steady standards and templates to increase the quality of knowledge content. This content may perhaps be in the form of clear and structured stages with shared framework of reference for project to enable flow of work necessitating least efforts and instruction hence decreasing 'Reinventing the wheel', lessening workload and augmenting profitability.

Another solution is the "checklist or risk registers" which contribute as 'living documents' (Antvik *et al.*,2009) (that turn into extensive and wide as the time passes and as a consequence of dynamic information feedback. Moreover, to enable the application of RM, expansion of activities to swap ideas inside teams and with other teams to influence conclusions by giving motivation and candidness to the greeting of diverse views deemed essential (Edwards *et al.*,2009).

As per the author's standpoint, one practical solution is to make more efficient and streamline the process of information assessment to root out the risks. This demands modest, operative systems and processes to develop novel information and content open to the end user as quickly as possible hence minimizing bottlenecks that shape the knowledge base more pertinent, valued, modernized and suitable that helps in the evaluation, refinement, and acceleration of the content and information formation process. The perception of KM and RM integration from this viewpoint is shortened in Figure 13.

The Technological Standpoint

As we all aware that the technology has major role to play on the other hand as stated in the literature review, it is not in-depth in its own terms. It operates along and nurtures networking and fraternity among the project team members operating in for RM. This can be in the form of creating functions for "COP's", establishing learning environments for strategic growth supported with intra/ internet, information sharing tools, self-learning, for

Figure 13. Concept for integrating KM into RM: The structural viewpoint

Figure 14. Concept for integrating KM into RM: The technological standpoint

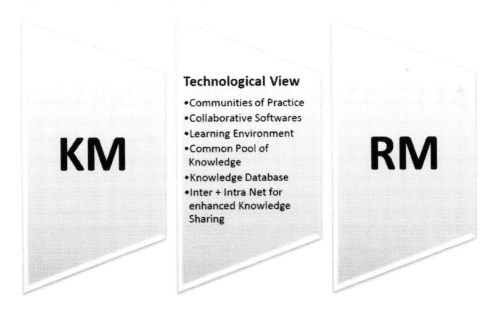

the facilitation of common group knowledge input and output, servers must be available, exchange of knowledge, techniques development for improving concerted approach to solve problems etc.

Such concepts can afterwards be developed to turn into the characteristics of KM that supports RM customization to the organizational structures and the level of existing ICT tools (Woodhead *et al.*,2000). These caters the purpose to encourage alliance, transparency and open access to information assets for viable project growth. As recommended in the interviews, the key emphasis must be on the employment of KM support systems instead of their mere formation. The perception of KM and RM integration from this viewpoint is shortened in Figure 14.

REFERENCES

Rebiasz, B. (2007). Fuzziness and randomness in investment project risk appraisal. *Computers & Operations Research, 34*(1), 199–210. doi:10.1016/j.cor.2005.05.006

Ringel-Bickelmaier, C., & Ringel, M. (2010). Knowledge management in international organisations. *Journal of Knowledge Management, 14*(4), 524-539. doi:10.1108/13673271011059509

Rodriguez, E., & Edwards, J. S. (2009). *Knowledge Management and Enterprise Risk Management Implementation in Financial Services.* Available at: http://www.ermsymposium.org/2009/pdf/2009-rodriguez-knowledge.pdf

Senge, P. (1990). *The Fifth Discipline: The art and practice of the learning organization.* New York: Doubleday.

Seyedhoseini, S. M., Noori, S., & Hatefi, M. A. (2009). An Integrated Methodology for Assessment and Selection of the Project Risk Response Actions. *Risk Analysis, 29*(5), 752-763. doi:10.1111/j.1539-6924.2008.01187.x

Shi, H., Li, W., & Meng, W. (2009). *A New Approach to Construction Project Risk Assessment Based on Rough Set and Information Entropy.* Paper presented at the ICIII '08. International Conference on Information Management, Innovation Management and Industrial Engineering, Taipei, Taiwan. Available at: http://ieeexplore.ieee.org/xpl/freeabs_all.jsp?arnumber=4737524

Spender, J. C. (2006). Getting value from knowledge management. *The TQM Magazine, 18*(3), 238–254. doi:10.1108/09544780610659970

Tiago, M. T. B., Couto, J. P. A., Tiago, F. G., & Vieira, J. A. C. (2007). Knowledge management: An overview of European reality. *Management Research News, 30*(2), 100-114. doi:10.1108/01409170710722946

UN. (2010). *Towards an accountability system in the United Nations Secretariat* (A/64/640). New York: United Nations. Available at: http://www.un.org/en/strengtheningtheun/pdf/A-64-640.pdf

UNESCO. (2009). *Risk Management: Evaluating, Managing and Mitigating Risk at UNESCO* (BPI/EPP/2009/PI/60M/14). UNESCO.

Conclusion

ACCOMPLISHMENT OF RESEARCH AIM

The research work has encompassed the reviewing and examination approaches of KM and RM and investigated and analyzed with a crucial standpoint as in what way these two dissimilar domains of Project Management can be united to benefit each other staring from the initial phases or stages of the project. The aim of this research work is achieved in terms of the examination and investigation of the magnitude to which the tools and techniques of KM can be made practical to the procedures and processes of RM utilized in the initial phases or stages of the projects. That has been confirmed and verified and the degree has been revealed to be extremely high with the analysis and recommendations to successfully device them for refining existing RM practices. The aim of the research work has also been achieved by attaining all four objectives that were presented in the start of the research work which are being elaborated in the forthcoming section.

Accomplishment of Research Objectives

The scope of this research work was presented abundantly precise and clear with breakdown of the aim into well-defined objectives. This smoothed and facilitated the exhaustive analysis and in-depth investigation of each and every defined objectives of the research while utilizing both the primary as well as the secondary research. The understanding of each and every objectives of the research is described below.

The first and foremost objective was to recognize the sources that are capable of creating the element of risk before and during the execution of the project. This has been inspected by virtue of the stretched literature review by examining the papers and reports published by international organizations and the results and recommendations of which were endorsed by virtue of primary research conducted in the shape of interview sessions with highly educated and experienced professional from varied project based organizations. During the research booth the primary as well as secondary data was thoroughly investigated and analyzed through a laborious methodical processes as elucidated in the early part of this research work. This unambiguously acknowledged the sources of risks existent in different stages of the project, they include: information unavailability, nonexistence of a mutually defined context, information flow is insufficient, absence of mutual framework of reference and Unproductive linkage systems. Such areas of risk have direct link with KM.

The second objective of the research work was to recognize and scrutinize the KM tools and techniques which can be utilized in different stages of the project. As the risks are deterring the projects at different stage of the project and has made obvious by virtue of the literature review as the secondary research with the verification and authentication with the help of primary research.. This conveyed an analysis in excess of which the tools and techniques might possibly be used for each of the known risks for dealing and minimize the impacts of the potential threats essential to the risks. It has been concluded that the KM tools and techniques are suitable to the procedure and processes of RM with specific devotion to the threats.

The third objective of the research work was to discover the commonalities between KM and RM tools and techniques as well as the conditions and situations below which the KM tools and techniques can be realistic to RM. This was pursued again by applying the points raised up in the earlier section and defining the areas in which the two domains presented the commonalities. The commonalities have been institute on unlike fronts which contain accumulation of knowledge, dissemination of knowledge, reprocessing of knowledge, collaboration as well as the problems encountered. This delivered complete picture of comprehension that these two domains were being utilized for the similar purpose but the context in which they applied is the only source of difference.

The fourth and the final objective of the research was to examine and analyze the sources of refining the RM tools and techniques applied in different stages of the project by applying KM approaches and strategies. This section reviewed the objective by dividing and segmenting the proposals into four sub- sections. These sub-sections of the research offer recommendations built on the learning experience gained by virtue of surveyed literature, the reports and the conducted interviews describing the suggestions and recommendations from the public's viewpoint, the outlook of context, the organizational structure standpoint and the viewpoint of technology.

Practical Implications of Research Work

This research work has transferred ideas into the comprehension level of two distinct domains of Project Management that are presently connected together by virtue of this study. It has delivered an understanding of how the embed the KM tools and techniques into RM and ultimately devise its execution. The gathering of primary data from various fields of PM enables the outputs and outcomes of the research are appropriate and hence applicable to the organization that have project based hierarchy. Consequently, the findings of the study can be exploited by the academicians and practitioners working with and dealing in the domains of Knowledge and Risk Management. In the academic circle, this can be made progressive to augment the standard tools and processes for KM and RM incorporation in the shape of a rich research by virtue of coalition between management professionals and university researchers.

The implication for social change of this research is from understanding the importance of managing the knowledge flow in an IT project and the different processes that are needed. The IT area of organizations provides systems for businesses, medical facilities, and government for social change. IT projects are helping with the supply of medical care to individuals who have not had it in the past. Government projects are becoming available for more people than in the past. IT projects are helping to create social change. As these IT projects are helping with social change, they are increasing the number of people involved and the need to interface with other computer systems. These complications have caused an increase in the knowledge sharing needed for the success of the IT projects. Finding ways to improve the knowledge sharing of the IT development process is the objective of this research. Understanding KM in the PM process for IT will help improve the process. With an improved PM process, better systems can be developed that can improve the lives of people in society.

Research Limitations

The scope of this research study, because of time constraints of the MS thesis, has been restricted to the investigation and examination of different stages of the only IT projects. As this literature review encompasses both the domains of RM and KM is all-inclusive and includes all the stages of the project, the study can be advanced from this stage ahead and hence can be applied for examination and investigation of different stages of the projects belong to different fields such as manufacturing, construction projects etc. This needs only the variety of extra data and information to be extracted from primary research which is pertinent and connected to different stages of the project. The assortment of more publications and reports obtained from the private sector can assist in the development of additional ideas and concepts that can be made realistic to that sector. The information obtained from the private sector was not made part of the current research because of the level confidentiality attached with these documents which controlled their usage in the research.

Future Research Directions

As far as the best knowledge of the author is concerned, the underlying research work presents one of the first efforts to discover the commonalities exist between the KM and RM domains of PM and their common alliance which leads PM research one step ahead and hence paves the way for future prospective research work. The research work has revealed the areas upon which this research work can be stretched for discovering extra deep and insightful relations between KM and RM. As presented in the discussion section, preferably KM and RM implemented together offers robust and strong foundation in order to handle the risks during the execution of the project. Hence, innovative techniques and approaches containing supplementary tools and techniques expending modern technological developments, that integrate both KM and RM strategies, can be definite and organized for linking all facets of the domains of KM and RM for the sake PM development.

Lastly, it is being concluded that an organization cannot succeed in managing its risk well until and unless the organization succeeds in managing its knowledge database. Effective amalgamation of both KM and RM tools and techniques can be accomplished by virtue of a well-adjusted collection of technology, fruitful work processes and adaptive mind set of the employees working in different capacities. Furthermore, the entire range of project process together with the project-based working practices necessities a standard change in thinking style. In the long run, the spirit of the whole issue is *"How can I know what I don't know I know?"*

Recommendations

The first recommendation for the first research question on KM for an IT project is to study other project-oriented areas outside of IT. Crawford and Pollack (2007) suggested that IT projects are similar to construction projects. IT projects are also similar to engineering and business development projects.

For the second research question on the tools used for IT projects success, further research is needed for the use of MS Access as a knowledge repository for business rules and standards for the organization. This was not predicted. Although there are some concerns about the database being in the development area, the tool is highly used and seems to be effective for the organization. Research is needed to find out whether other organizations use this type of tool for KM to share business knowledge between users and the IT area. Is the tool used for business rules and standards? What is the user's role in maintaining this system?

The third research question focused on the current PM process for managing knowledge. Further research is needed for this question based upon the research by the author of (Emblemm *et al.*,2010), and comparing the PM process with the process of the insurance organization. This research was similar to (Emblemm *et al.*,2010), study on knowledge sharing. The research showed a high quality of information being shared within the project and a high number of shared resources between projects. During the interviews, project team members of one group seemed to be very familiar with the other current projects. The reason for this seemed to be the design reviews and quality control processing within the IT area. Design reviews were open to any member of the IT area who wished to join the meeting. Besides making the design standards for the organization known, it also helped keep all members of the IT area informed about the other projects in the organization.

CONCLUSION

In the research, it was found that the traditional KM and RM tools were being integrated together to combine the knowledge of the team members for better risk assessment of IT projects. Ten different of risks that have the potential to affect the flow of IT project at any stage of development life cycle can be mitigated by effective and efficient use of KM techniques. As the research results are based on the experiences of highly experienced and well qualified IT professionals of public and corporate sector of Pakistan this results and suggestions can be equally applicable to any organization operating in any domain and any part of the world.

REFERENCES

Uriarte, F. A., Jr. (2008). Introduction to Knowledge Management. Jakarta: ASEAN Foundation.

Vargas, R. (2009). *The History of Risk Management*. Available at: http://www.slideshare.net/ricardo.vargas/ricardo-vargas-historico-gerenciamento-riscos-ppt-en

Web Finance. (2012). *Business Dictionary*. Available at: http://www.businessdictionary.com/definition/knowledge.html

WHO. (2006). *Bridging the "Know–Do" Gap*. Geneva: World Health Organization.

Wickboldt, J. A., Bianchin, L. A., Lunardi, R. C., Granville, L. Z., Gaspary, L. P., & Bartolini, C. (2011). A framework for risk assessment based on analysis of historical information of workflow execution in IT systems. *Computer Networks, 55*(13), 2957–2975. doi:10.1016/j.comnet.2011.05.025

Woodhead, R. M. (2000). Investigation of the early stages of project formulation. *Facilities, 18*(14), 524-534. doi:10.1108/02632770010358079

Zhang, H. (2007). A redefinition of the project risk process: Using vulnerability to open up the event-consequence link. *International Journal of Project Management, 25*(7), 694–701. doi:10.1016/j.ijproman.2007.02.004

Zhang, K., Zhang, R., & Zhang, X.-L. (2010). *Research on the Influence of Knowledge Management Capability to Intellectual Property Risk in Enterprise Independent Innovation*. Paper presented at the International Conference on E-Business and E-Government, Guangzho, China.

Appendix

LIST OF ABBREVIATIONS

AAR: After Action Reviews
APM: Association for Project Management
APMBOK: APM Body of Knowledge
BM: Benchmarking
BS: Brainstorming Session
CKO: Chief Knowledge Officer
COP: Communities of Practice
DMS: Document Management Systems
DSS: Decision Support Systems
EL: Expertise Locator
FAQ: Frequently Asked Questions
IM: Information Management
ICT: Information and Communications Technology
ISO: International Organization for Standardization
KA: Knowledge Audit
KF: Knowledge Fair
KM: Knowledge Management
KMS: Knowledge Management Systems
OECD: Organization for Economic Co-operation and Development
PESTEL: Political, Environmental, Social, Technical, Economic, Legal
PKM: Project Knowledge Management
PM: Project Management
PMBOK: Project Management Body of Knowledge
PRM: Project Risk Management
RBS: Risk Breakdown Structure
RM: Risk Management
SWOT: Strengths, Weaknesses, Opportunities, Threats

UN: United Nations
UNESCO: United Nations Educational, Scientific and Cultural Organization
UNO: United Nations Organization
WHO: World Health Organization

INTERVIEW TEMPLATE

1.   Name of Interviewer:
2.   Date of Interview session:
3.   Name of Interviewee:
4.   Gender:
5.   Age Group:
     a.   36-40 Years
     b.   41-45 Years
     c.   46-50 Years
     d.   51-55 Years
     e.   56-60 Years
     f.   61+
6.   Current Appointment / Designation:
7.   Qualification:
8.   Professional Experience (in years):
9.   Name of Present Employer/ Organization:

Segment No 1 Questions

RQ1: In what way a KM be used in PM for IT projects?
RQ2: In what way are the tools and techniques for KM used in IT PM to increase the success rate of an IT project?
RQ3: In what way the existing PM process handling knowledge for an IT project?
RQ4: In what way does the PKM model for handling knowledge improve the success of an IT project?

Segment No 2 Questions

RQ5: To what extent, in your esteemed organization, the KM practices are developed or mature?

RQ6: In what manner would you describe the application or utilization of KM in your esteemed organization?

RQ7: Do your organization has any documented policy as far KM tools & techniques are concerned?

RQ8: At what extent your organization practices the tools, techniques or methods (Storytelling, Benchmarking, Brainstorming etc.) for KM?

RQ9: At what extent your organization practices the tools, techniques or methods (SWOT, PESTEL, FMEA etc.) for RM?

Segment No 3 Questions

RQ10: To what extent the sources of risk (like information unavailability, inappropriate flow of information etc.) affects your esteemed organization?

Segment No 4 Questions

RRQ11: In your viewpoint how the techniques and approaches of KM & RM share similarities?

Segment No 5 Questions

RQ12: In your perspective, is there any scope available for incorporating KM tool & techniques into RM tool & techniques?

RQ13: Would you like to give any suggestions / recommendations for KM and RM as well as for joint functioning?

Related Readings

To continue IGI Global's long-standing tradition of advancing innovation through emerging research, please find below a compiled list of recommended IGI Global book chapters and journal articles in the areas of knowledge management, information technology, and project management. These related readings will provide additional information and guidance to further enrich your knowledge and assist you with your own research.

Aagaard, A. (2019). Knowledge Management Strategy Implementation Through Knowledge Ambassadors. In M. Jennex (Ed.), *Effective Knowledge Management Systems in Modern Society* (pp. 193–211). Hershey, PA: IGI Global. doi:10.4018/978-1-5225-5427-1.ch010

Abdelhamid, M., Venkatesan, S., Gaia, J., & Sharman, R. (2018). Do Privacy Concerns Affect Information Seeking via Smartphones? In M. Gupta, R. Sharman, J. Walp, & P. Mulgund (Eds.), *Information Technology Risk Management and Compliance in Modern Organizations* (pp. 301–314). Hershey, PA: IGI Global. doi:10.4018/978-1-5225-2604-9.ch011

Aiello, L., & Gatti, M. (2017). Project Portfolio Management and Organization: An Integrated and Circular Model. In L. Romano (Ed.), *Project Portfolio Management Strategies for Effective Organizational Operations* (pp. 288–309). Hershey, PA: IGI Global. doi:10.4018/978-1-5225-2151-8.ch012

Al-Rousan, T., & Abualese, H. (2018). The Importance of Process Improvement in Web-Based Projects. In T. Bagwell, R. Cropf, & S. Foster-Gadkari (Eds.), *Information Technology as a Facilitator of Social Processes in Project Management and Collaborative Work* (pp. 62–82). Hershey, PA: IGI Global. doi:10.4018/978-1-5225-3471-6.ch004

Alhawari, S., Jarrah, M. A., & Hadi, W. (2017). Implementing Risk Management Processes into a Cloud Computing Environment. *International Journal of Web Portals*, *9*(1), 1–12. doi:10.4018/IJWP.2017010101

Alkhuraiji, A. I. (2018). The Influence of the Top Management Characteristics on the Success of the Enterprise Information System. In A. Borchers (Ed.), *Technology Management in Organizational and Societal Contexts* (pp. 1–26). Hershey, PA: IGI Global. doi:10.4018/978-1-5225-5279-6.ch001

Amaral, A. M., & Araújo, M. (2017). Project Portfolio Selection Using a D.E.A. Approach. In L. Romano (Ed.), *Project Portfolio Management Strategies for Effective Organizational Operations* (pp. 220–244). Hershey, PA: IGI Global. doi:10.4018/978-1-5225-2151-8.ch009

Anderson, R., & Mansingh, G. (2019). CoMIS-KMS: An Elaborated Process Model for Transitioning MIS to KMS. In M. Jennex (Ed.), *Effective Knowledge Management Systems in Modern Society* (pp. 171–192). Hershey, PA: IGI Global. doi:10.4018/978-1-5225-5427-1.ch009

Aparo von Flüe, A. (2017). Are You Pondering What I Am Pondering?: Eccentric Consideration on Strategic Management. In L. Romano (Ed.), *Project Portfolio Management Strategies for Effective Organizational Operations* (pp. 81–118). Hershey, PA: IGI Global. doi:10.4018/978-1-5225-2151-8.ch004

Archibald, R. D. (2017). Inter-Relationships between an Enterprise's Strategic Management Process and Its Program/Project Portfolio Management Process. In L. Romano (Ed.), *Project Portfolio Management Strategies for Effective Organizational Operations* (pp. 39–60). Hershey, PA: IGI Global. doi:10.4018/978-1-5225-2151-8.ch002

Bandera, C., Passerini, K., & Bartolacci, M. R. (2019). Knowledge Management and Entrepreneurship Research and Practice: Status, Challenges, and Opportunities. In M. Jennex (Ed.), *Effective Knowledge Management Systems in Modern Society* (pp. 45–61). Hershey, PA: IGI Global. doi:10.4018/978-1-5225-5427-1.ch003

Bashayreh, A. M. (2018). Organizational Culture and Organizational Performance. In W. Lee & F. Sabetzadeh (Eds.), *Contemporary Knowledge and Systems Science* (pp. 50–69). Hershey, PA: IGI Global. doi:10.4018/978-1-5225-5655-8.ch003

Bernardes, S., Leite, P., Pesenti, G. S., Viana, E. A., Ladeira, V., Castro, C., ... Renato de Sousa, P. (2017). Information Management Applied to the Development of the Management Process and Improving Energy Efficiency in Transport. In G. Jamil, A. Soares, & C. Pessoa (Eds.), *Handbook of Research on Information Management for Effective Logistics and Supply Chains* (pp. 166–179). Hershey, PA: IGI Global. doi:10.4018/978-1-5225-0973-8.ch009

Bhattacharjee, J., Sengupta, A., Barik, M. S., & Mazumdar, C. (2018). An Analytical Study of Methodologies and Tools for Enterprise Information Security Risk Management. In M. Gupta, R. Sharman, J. Walp, & P. Mulgund (Eds.), *Information Technology Risk Management and Compliance in Modern Organizations* (pp. 1–20). Hershey, PA: IGI Global. doi:10.4018/978-1-5225-2604-9.ch001

Bhattacharya, P. J. (2018). Managing IT to Innovate and Strategize in the Higher Education Sector: Role of Enterprise Systems. In A. Borchers (Ed.), *Technology Management in Organizational and Societal Contexts* (pp. 27–50). Hershey, PA: IGI Global. doi:10.4018/978-1-5225-5279-6.ch002

Bruno, G. (2017). Identification of Potential Clients, Providers, and Competitors in Supply Chain Networks. In G. Jamil, A. Soares, & C. Pessoa (Eds.), *Handbook of Research on Information Management for Effective Logistics and Supply Chains* (pp. 89–106). Hershey, PA: IGI Global. doi:10.4018/978-1-5225-0973-8.ch005

Bucero, A. (2017). Linking Organization's Strategy and Strategic Planning with Portfolio Management. In L. Romano (Ed.), *Project Portfolio Management Strategies for Effective Organizational Operations* (pp. 61–80). Hershey, PA: IGI Global. doi:10.4018/978-1-5225-2151-8.ch003

Budu, J. (2018). Applying Agile Principles in Teaching Undergraduate Information Technology Project Management. *International Journal of Information and Communication Technology Education, 14*(3), 29–40. doi:10.4018/IJICTE.2018070103

Bushuyev, S., & Verenych, O. (2018). Organizational Maturity and Project: Program and Portfolio Success. In G. Silvius & G. Karayaz (Eds.), *Developing Organizational Maturity for Effective Project Management* (pp. 104–127). Hershey, PA: IGI Global. doi:10.4018/978-1-5225-3197-5.ch006

Capatina, A., Vasilache, R., Schin, G. C., & Antohi, V. M. (2018). Drivers and Barriers Related to Project Management Software Implementation in Romanian Organizations: A Force Field Analysis. In T. Bagwell, R. Cropf, & S. Foster-Gadkari (Eds.), *Information Technology as a Facilitator of Social Processes in Project Management and Collaborative Work* (pp. 40–61). Hershey, PA: IGI Global. doi:10.4018/978-1-5225-3471-6.ch003

Catania, C. A., Zanni-Merk, C., Bertrand de Beuvron, F. D., & Collet, P. (2018). Knowledge-Intensive Evolutionary Algorithms for Solving a Healthcare Fleet Optimization Problem: An Ontological Approach. In W. Lee & F. Sabetzadeh (Eds.), *Contemporary Knowledge and Systems Science* (pp. 192–223). Hershey, PA: IGI Global. doi:10.4018/978-1-5225-5655-8.ch008

Celestine, N. A., & Perryer, C. (2019). The Determinants of Interorganizational Knowledge Coaching Success: Looking Ahead to the Future of Knowledge Transfer. In M. Jennex (Ed.), *Effective Knowledge Management Systems in Modern Society* (pp. 146–169). Hershey, PA: IGI Global. doi:10.4018/978-1-5225-5427-1.ch008

Chaudhari, G., & Mulgund, P. (2018). Strengthening IT Governance With COBIT 5. In M. Gupta, R. Sharman, J. Walp, & P. Mulgund (Eds.), *Information Technology Risk Management and Compliance in Modern Organizations* (pp. 48–69). Hershey, PA: IGI Global. doi:10.4018/978-1-5225-2604-9.ch003

Costa, E., Soares, A. L., Pinho de Sousa, J., & Jamil, G. L. (2017). Information Management for Network Transformation in Industrial Enterprises Associations: The Case of the Internationalization Process. In G. Jamil, A. Soares, & C. Pessoa (Eds.), *Handbook of Research on Information Management for Effective Logistics and Supply Chains* (pp. 415–436). Hershey, PA: IGI Global. doi:10.4018/978-1-5225-0973-8.ch022

Daza, R., & Hargiss, K. M. (2018). Factors Comprising Effective Risk Communication, Decision-Making, and Measurement of IT and IA Risk. *International Journal of Strategic Information Technology and Applications*, 9(1), 23–40. doi:10.4018/IJSITA.2018010102 de Heer, K., Lok, H., & Schouten, T. (2018). Insight in Changeability as a Success Factor for Projects: Assessing the Change Capacity of an Organization. In G. Silvius & G. Karayaz (Eds.), *Developing Organizational Maturity for Effective Project Management* (pp. 210–231). Hershey, PA: IGI Global. doi:10.4018/978-1-5225-3197-5.ch011

Duarte, M., Baptista, A., & Pinto, G. (2018). Learning in the Laboratory: Accessing Videos With Quick Response Codes. In A. Borchers (Ed.), *Technology Management in Organizational and Societal Contexts* (pp. 117–138). Hershey, PA: IGI Global. doi:10.4018/978-1-5225-5279-6.ch006

Durst, S., Bruns, G., & Edvardsson, I. R. (2018). Knowledge Retention in Smaller Firms. In W. Lee & F. Sabetzadeh (Eds.), *Contemporary Knowledge and Systems Science* (pp. 100–119). Hershey, PA: IGI Global. doi:10.4018/978-1-5225-5655-8.ch005

Durst, S., Bruns, G., & Henschel, T. (2016). The Management of Knowledge Risks: What do We Really Know? *International Journal of Knowledge and Systems Science*, 7(3), 19–29. doi:10.4018/IJKSS.2016070102

Endres, M. L., & Chowdhury, S. (2019). Team and Individual Interactions With Reciprocity in Individual Knowledge Sharing. In M. Jennex (Ed.), *Effective Knowledge Management Systems in Modern Society* (pp. 123–145). Hershey, PA: IGI Global. doi:10.4018/978-1-5225-5427-1.ch007

Fernandes da Anunciação, P., Garcia, B., & Fonseca, G. (2017). Importance of Stakeholders Identification in Information Distribution Chain Management for Public Value Detection in Public Initiatives. In G. Jamil, A. Soares, & C. Pessoa (Eds.), *Handbook of Research on Information Management for Effective Logistics and Supply Chains* (pp. 131–146). Hershey, PA: IGI Global. doi:10.4018/978-1-5225-0973-8.ch007

Fernandes da Anunciação, P., Lobo, M., Pereira, O., & Mateus, G. (2017). The Importance of Perception and Appreciation of the Information Management for Effective Logistics and Supply Chain in Transport Sector. In G. Jamil, A. Soares, & C. Pessoa (Eds.), *Handbook of Research on Information Management for Effective Logistics and Supply Chains* (pp. 453–468). Hershey, PA: IGI Global. doi:10.4018/978-1-5225-0973-8.ch024

Fernandes da Anunciação, P., Zambon, A. C., Andrade, F. D., & Sanches de Sousa, C. S. (2017). Competitive Intelligence Competitive Intelligence: A Proposal for Value Creation through Information and Knowledge – The Limeira Gross Domestic Product Sector: Brazil. In G. Jamil, A. Soares, & C. Pessoa (Eds.), *Handbook of Research on Information Management for Effective Logistics and Supply Chains* (pp. 273–286). Hershey, PA: IGI Global. doi:10.4018/978-1-5225-0973-8.ch015

Fonseca, G. L., Rodello, I. A., & Fernandes da Anunciação, P. (2017). Information Management and Enterprise Resource Planning: An Analysis of the Medical Products Distribution Chain. In G. Jamil, A. Soares, & C. Pessoa (Eds.), *Handbook of Research on Information Management for Effective Logistics and Supply Chains* (pp. 334–349). Hershey, PA: IGI Global. doi:10.4018/978-1-5225-0973-8.ch019

Galli, B. J. (2018). Continuous Improvement Relationship to Risk Management: The Relationship Between Them. *International Journal of Applied Management Sciences and Engineering*, 5(2), 1–14. doi:10.4018/IJAMSE.2018070101

Gan, R. C., & Chin, C. M. (2018). Components of Project Management Maturity Impacting Project, Program, Portfolio, and Organizational Success. In G. Silvius & G. Karayaz (Eds.), *Developing Organizational Maturity for Effective Project Management* (pp. 128–152). Hershey, PA: IGI Global. doi:10.4018/978-1-5225-3197-5.ch007

Garling, R. (2018). Does an Open Source Development Environment Facilitate Conventional Project Management Approaches and Collaborative Work? In T. Bagwell, R. Cropf, & S. Foster-Gadkari (Eds.), *Information Technology as a Facilitator of Social Processes in Project Management and Collaborative Work* (pp. 99–123). Hershey, PA: IGI Global. doi:10.4018/978-1-5225-3471-6.ch006

Gloet, M., & Samson, D. (2019). Knowledge and Innovation Management: Creating Value. In M. Jennex (Ed.), *Effective Knowledge Management Systems in Modern Society* (pp. 19–44). Hershey, PA: IGI Global. doi:10.4018/978-1-5225-5427-1.ch002

Gumz, J. (2017). Managing Change: Strategies and Tactics to Review the Portfolio. In L. Romano (Ed.), *Project Portfolio Management Strategies for Effective Organizational Operations* (pp. 334–357). Hershey, PA: IGI Global. doi:10.4018/978-1-5225-2151-8.ch014

Gupta, D. S., & Biswas, G. P. (2018). On Securing Cloud Storage Using a Homomorphic Framework. In A. Borchers (Ed.), *Technology Management in Organizational and Societal Contexts* (pp. 99–114). Hershey, PA: IGI Global. doi:10.4018/978-1-5225-5279-6.ch005

Herrera, J. E., Argüello, L. V., Gonzalez-Feliu, J., & Jaimes, W. A. (2017). Decision Support System Design Requirements, Information Management, and Urban Logistics Efficiency: Case Study of Bogotá, Colombia. In G. Jamil, A. Soares, & C. Pessoa (Eds.), *Handbook of Research on Information Management for Effective Logistics and Supply Chains* (pp. 223–238). Hershey, PA: IGI Global. doi:10.4018/978-1-5225-0973-8.ch012

Iltchev, P., Palczewska, A., Pilichowska, K., Kozlowski, R., & Marczak, M. (2017). Benefits of the Transics Fleet Management System. In G. Jamil, A. Soares, & C. Pessoa (Eds.), *Handbook of Research on Information Management for Effective Logistics and Supply Chains* (pp. 287–302). Hershey, PA: IGI Global. doi:10.4018/978-1-5225-0973-8.ch016

Ilvonen, I., Jussila, J., & Kärkkäinen, H. (2019). A Business-Driven Process Model for Knowledge Security Risk Management: Tackling Knowledge Risks While Realizing Business Benefits. In M. Jennex (Ed.), *Effective Knowledge Management Systems in Modern Society* (pp. 308–325). Hershey, PA: IGI Global. doi:10.4018/978-1-5225-5427-1.ch015

Jamil, G. L. (2017). Numbers Can Restrict Results?: Qualitative Research Methods as Information and Knowledge Management Support in Supply Chain and Logistics Sectors. In G. Jamil, A. Soares, & C. Pessoa (Eds.), *Handbook of Research on Information Management for Effective Logistics and Supply Chains* (pp. 1–22). Hershey, PA: IGI Global. doi:10.4018/978-1-5225-0973-8.ch001

Jamil, G. L., & Jamil, C. C. (2017). Information and Knowledge Management Perspective Contributions for Fashion Studies: Observing Logistics and Supply Chain Management Processes. In G. Jamil, A. Soares, & C. Pessoa (Eds.), *Handbook of Research on Information Management for Effective Logistics and Supply Chains* (pp. 199–221). Hershey, PA: IGI Global. doi:10.4018/978-1-5225-0973-8.ch011

Janssens, J. (2018). Project and Portfolio Maturity for Waterfall and Agile: Convergence of Layered Needs in Different Ecosystems. In G. Silvius & G. Karayaz (Eds.), *Developing Organizational Maturity for Effective Project Management* (pp. 253–277). Hershey, PA: IGI Global. doi:10.4018/978-1-5225-3197-5.ch013

Jennex, M. E. (2019). Using a Revised Knowledge Pyramid to Redefine Knowledge Management Strategy. In M. Jennex (Ed.), *Effective Knowledge Management Systems in Modern Society* (pp. 1–18). Hershey, PA: IGI Global. doi:10.4018/978-1-5225-5427-1.ch001

Jennex, M. E., & Durcikova, A. (2019). Integrating IS Security With Knowledge Management: What Can Knowledge Management Learn From IS Security Vice Versa? In M. Jennex (Ed.), *Effective Knowledge Management Systems in Modern Society* (pp. 267–283). Hershey, PA: IGI Global. doi:10.4018/978-1-5225-5427-1.ch013

Johnson, R. D., Adkins, J., & Pepper, D. (2018). Project-Based Organizational Maturity in Architecture, Engineering, and Construction: A Theoretical Premise for Practical Purposes. In G. Silvius & G. Karayaz (Eds.), *Developing Organizational Maturity for Effective Project Management* (pp. 55–77). Hershey, PA: IGI Global. doi:10.4018/978-1-5225-3197-5.ch004

Jridi, K., Jaziri-Bouagina, D., & Triki, A. (2017). The SCM, CRM Information System, and KM – An Integrating Theoretical View: The Case of Sales Force Automation. In G. Jamil, A. Soares, & C. Pessoa (Eds.), *Handbook of Research on Information Management for Effective Logistics and Supply Chains* (pp. 239–254). Hershey, PA: IGI Global. doi:10.4018/978-1-5225-0973-8.ch013

Kasemsap, K. (2017). Advocating Information System, Information Integration, and Information Sharing in Global Supply Chain. In G. Jamil, A. Soares, & C. Pessoa (Eds.), *Handbook of Research on Information Management for Effective Logistics and Supply Chains* (pp. 107–130). Hershey, PA: IGI Global. doi:10.4018/978-1-5225-0973-8.ch006

Keil, A., Friedrich, R., & Doppelfeld, D. (2018). Organizational Success and Failure Criteria in Virtual Team Maturity. In G. Silvius & G. Karayaz (Eds.), *Developing Organizational Maturity for Effective Project Management* (pp. 169–200). Hershey, PA: IGI Global. doi:10.4018/978-1-5225-3197-5.ch009

Kisielnicki, J., & Sobolewska, O. (2019). *Knowledge Management and Innovation in Network Organizations: Emerging Research and Opportunities* (pp. 1–187). Hershey, PA: IGI Global. doi:10.4018/978-1-5225-5930-6

Kozlowski, R., Iltchev, P., Palczewska, A., Pilichowska, K., & Marczak, M. (2017). Analysis of the Possibility to Implement the Transics System and GBOX Assist Systems in a Selected Company. In G. Jamil, A. Soares, & C. Pessoa (Eds.), *Handbook of Research on Information Management for Effective Logistics and Supply Chains* (pp. 303–315). Hershey, PA: IGI Global. doi:10.4018/978-1-5225-0973-8.ch017

Krishnamachariar, P. K., & Gupta, M. (2018). Swimming Upstream in Turbulent Waters: Auditing Agile Development. In M. Gupta, R. Sharman, J. Walp, & P. Mulgund (Eds.), *Information Technology Risk Management and Compliance in Modern Organizations* (pp. 268–300). Hershey, PA: IGI Global. doi:10.4018/978-1-5225-2604-9.ch010

Lahmiri, S. (2018). Information Technology Outsourcing Risk Factors and Provider Selection. In M. Gupta, R. Sharman, J. Walp, & P. Mulgund (Eds.), *Information Technology Risk Management and Compliance in Modern Organizations* (pp. 214–228). Hershey, PA: IGI Global. doi:10.4018/978-1-5225-2604-9.ch008

Lazzareschi, V. H., & Brito, M. S. (2017). Strategic Information Management: Proposal of Business Project Model. In G. Jamil, A. Soares, & C. Pessoa (Eds.), *Handbook of Research on Information Management for Effective Logistics and Supply Chains* (pp. 59–88). Hershey, PA: IGI Global. doi:10.4018/978-1-5225-0973-8.ch004

Levin, G., & Pitotti, N. (2017). Program and Portfolio Management Relationship and Support. In L. Romano (Ed.), *Project Portfolio Management Strategies for Effective Organizational Operations* (pp. 310–333). Hershey, PA: IGI Global. doi:10.4018/978-1-5225-2151-8.ch013

Lima de Magalhães, J., & Moreira, A. (2017). Information Systems Management in the Supply Chain in an Official Pharmaceutical Laboratory. In G. Jamil, A. Soares, & C. Pessoa (Eds.), *Handbook of Research on Information Management for Effective Logistics and Supply Chains* (pp. 350–373). Hershey, PA: IGI Global. doi:10.4018/978-1-5225-0973-8.ch020

Lofaro, R. J. (2019). Knowledge Engineering, Cognitive Ergonomics, and Knowledge Management in 2017: A New Delphi Paradigm With Applications. In M. Jennex (Ed.), *Effective Knowledge Management Systems in Modern Society* (pp. 78–97). Hershey, PA: IGI Global. doi:10.4018/978-1-5225-5427-1.ch005

Loganathan, S. (2018). A Step-by-Step Procedural Methodology for Improving an Organization's IT Risk Management System. In M. Gupta, R. Sharman, J. Walp, & P. Mulgund (Eds.), *Information Technology Risk Management and Compliance in Modern Organizations* (pp. 21–47). Hershey, PA: IGI Global. doi:10.4018/978-1-5225-2604-9.ch002

Lopes, B., Falcão, L., & Canellas, T. (2017). Supply-Side: Mapping High Capacity Suppliers of Goods and Services. In G. Jamil, A. Soares, & C. Pessoa (Eds.), *Handbook of Research on Information Management for Effective Logistics and Supply Chains* (pp. 147–165). Hershey, PA: IGI Global. doi:10.4018/978-1-5225-0973-8.ch008

Loya, V. M., Alcaraz, J. L., Reza, J. R., & Gayosso, D. G. (2017). The Impact of ICT on Supply Chain Agility and Human Performance. In G. Jamil, A. Soares, & C. Pessoa (Eds.), *Handbook of Research on Information Management for Effective Logistics and Supply Chains* (pp. 180–198). Hershey, PA: IGI Global. doi:10.4018/978-1-5225-0973-8.ch010

Manchado-Pérez, E., López-Forniés, I., & Berges-Muro, L. (2018). Value of Adaptation of Methodologies Between Different Knowledge Areas: As Applied in the Context of Project-Based Learning. In A. Borchers (Ed.), *Technology Management in Organizational and Societal Contexts* (pp. 221–248). Hershey, PA: IGI Global. doi:10.4018/978-1-5225-5279-6.ch010

Manh, T. N. (2018). A Systems Theory of Organizational Information. In W. Lee & F. Sabetzadeh (Eds.), *Contemporary Knowledge and Systems Science* (pp. 1–37). Hershey, PA: IGI Global. doi:10.4018/978-1-5225-5655-8.ch001

Maranga, K. (2018). Virtual Organizations and IT Project Management. In T. Bagwell, R. Cropf, & S. Foster-Gadkari (Eds.), *Information Technology as a Facilitator of Social Processes in Project Management and Collaborative Work* (pp. 144–157). Hershey, PA: IGI Global. doi:10.4018/978-1-5225-3471-6.ch008

Marnewick, C., & Langerman, J. (2018). Agile Maturity: The First Step to Information Technology Project Success. In G. Silvius & G. Karayaz (Eds.), *Developing Organizational Maturity for Effective Project Management* (pp. 233–252). Hershey, PA: IGI Global. doi:10.4018/978-1-5225-3197-5.ch012

McKay, D. S., & Ellis, T. J. (2019). Measuring the Relationship Among Learning Enablers and IT Project Success. In M. Jennex (Ed.), *Effective Knowledge Management Systems in Modern Society* (pp. 212–235). Hershey, PA: IGI Global. doi:10.4018/978-1-5225-5427-1.ch011

Messina, D., Santos, C., Soares, A. L., & Barros, A. C. (2017). Risk and Visibility in Supply Chains: An Information Management Perspective. In G. Jamil, A. Soares, & C. Pessoa (Eds.), *Handbook of Research on Information Management for Effective Logistics and Supply Chains* (pp. 34–57). Hershey, PA: IGI Global. doi:10.4018/978-1-5225-0973-8.ch003

Moshonsky, M., Serenko, A., & Bontis, N. (2019). Practical Relevance of Management Research: The Role of Doctoral Program Graduates. In M. Jennex (Ed.), *Effective Knowledge Management Systems in Modern Society* (pp. 236–265). Hershey, PA: IGI Global. doi:10.4018/978-1-5225-5427-1.ch012

Nabavi, A., Taghavi-Fard, M. T., Hanafizadeh, P., & Taghva, M. R. (2016). Information Technology Continuance Intention: A Systematic Literature Review. *International Journal of E-Business Research*, *12*(1), 58–95. doi:10.4018/IJEBR.2016010104

Nachbagauer, A. G., & Schirl-Boeck, I. B. (2018). Organizational Maturity Beyond Risk Management: Successfully Managing the Unexpected. In G. Silvius & G. Karayaz (Eds.), *Developing Organizational Maturity for Effective Project Management* (pp. 78–103). Hershey, PA: IGI Global. doi:10.4018/978-1-5225-3197-5.ch005

Nakamori, Y., Meng, F., & Huynh, V. (2018). Knowledge-Scientific Evaluation of Social Service Systems. In W. Lee & F. Sabetzadeh (Eds.), *Contemporary Knowledge and Systems Science* (pp. 120–150). Hershey, PA: IGI Global. doi:10.4018/978-1-5225-5655-8.ch006

Nakamori, Y., Sun, J., Wu, J., Tian, J., & Huynh, V. (2018). A Knowledge Creation Model for Graduate Research. In W. Lee & F. Sabetzadeh (Eds.), *Contemporary Knowledge and Systems Science* (pp. 70–99). Hershey, PA: IGI Global. doi:10.4018/978-1-5225-5655-8.ch004

Nanda, A., Popat, P., & Vimalkumar, D. (2018). Navigating Through Choppy Waters of PCI DSS Compliance. In M. Gupta, R. Sharman, J. Walp, & P. Mulgund (Eds.), *Information Technology Risk Management and Compliance in Modern Organizations* (pp. 99–140). Hershey, PA: IGI Global. doi:10.4018/978-1-5225-2604-9.ch005

Narayanan, V. K. (2018). Elaborating the Project Management System: Influence on Project Managers. In G. Silvius & G. Karayaz (Eds.), *Developing Organizational Maturity for Effective Project Management* (pp. 25–42). Hershey, PA: IGI Global. doi:10.4018/978-1-5225-3197-5.ch002

Nonino, F. (2017). Project Selection Frameworks and Methodologies for Reducing Risks in Project Portfolio Management. In L. Romano (Ed.), *Project Portfolio Management Strategies for Effective Organizational Operations* (pp. 245–263). Hershey, PA: IGI Global. doi:10.4018/978-1-5225-2151-8.ch010

Nylund, P. A., Arimany-Serrat, N., Ferràs-Hernández, X., & Corral-Marfil, J. A. (2018). Home Bias in Innovation Ecosystems: Relying on Local Users for Knowledge. In A. Borchers (Ed.), *Technology Management in Organizational and Societal Contexts* (pp. 78–97). Hershey, PA: IGI Global. doi:10.4018/978-1-5225-5279-6.ch004

Olson, B. (2017). Optimizing Portfolio Value through Comprehensive Project Metrics. In L. Romano (Ed.), *Project Portfolio Management Strategies for Effective Organizational Operations* (pp. 178–201). Hershey, PA: IGI Global. doi:10.4018/978-1-5225-2151-8.ch007

Özen, Z., Kartal, E., & Emre, İ. E. (2018). Analysis of a Learning Management System by Using Google Analytics: A Case Study From Turkey. In A. Borchers (Ed.), *Technology Management in Organizational and Societal Contexts* (pp. 198–220). Hershey, PA: IGI Global. doi:10.4018/978-1-5225-5279-6.ch009

Ozlen, K., & Handzic, M. (2019). A Contingency Perspective for Knowledge Management Solutions in Different Decision-Making Contexts. In M. Jennex (Ed.), *Effective Knowledge Management Systems in Modern Society* (pp. 62–77). Hershey, PA: IGI Global. doi:10.4018/978-1-5225-5427-1.ch004

Paliktzoglou, V., & Suhonen, J. (2018). Microblogging Case Study in Higher Education: Edmodo in Finland. In A. Borchers (Ed.), *Technology Management in Organizational and Societal Contexts* (pp. 139–168). Hershey, PA: IGI Global. doi:10.4018/978-1-5225-5279-6.ch007

Parry, V. K., & Lind, M. L. (2016). Alignment of Business Strategy and Information Technology Considering Information Technology Governance, Project Portfolio Control, and Risk Management. *International Journal of Information Technology Project Management*, 7(4), 21–37. doi:10.4018/IJITPM.2016100102

Parth, F. R. (2017). Preparing the Organization for Portfolio Management: Overcoming Resistance and Obstacles. In L. Romano (Ed.), *Project Portfolio Management Strategies for Effective Organizational Operations* (pp. 119–152). Hershey, PA: IGI Global. doi:10.4018/978-1-5225-2151-8.ch005

Parth, F. R. (2017). Project Portfolio Management Growth and Operation: Portfolio Management Structure, Operations, Risk, and Growth. In L. Romano (Ed.), *Project Portfolio Management Strategies for Effective Organizational Operations* (pp. 264–287). Hershey, PA: IGI Global. doi:10.4018/978-1-5225-2151-8.ch011

Pasian, B. (2018). Project Management Maturity and Associated Modeling: A Historic, Process-Oriented View. In G. Silvius & G. Karayaz (Eds.), *Developing Organizational Maturity for Effective Project Management* (pp. 1–24). Hershey, PA: IGI Global. doi:10.4018/978-1-5225-3197-5.ch001

Pattabiraman, A., Srinivasan, S., Swaminathan, K., & Gupta, M. (2018). Fortifying Corporate Human Wall: A Literature Review of Security Awareness and Training. In M. Gupta, R. Sharman, J. Walp, & P. Mulgund (Eds.), *Information Technology Risk Management and Compliance in Modern Organizations* (pp. 142–175). Hershey, PA: IGI Global. doi:10.4018/978-1-5225-2604-9.ch006

Peixoto, J., Tereso, A., Fernandes, G., & Almeida, R. (2016). A Project Risk Management Methodology Developed for an Electrical Portuguese Organization. *International Journal of Human Capital and Information Technology Professionals*, 7(1), 1–19. doi:10.4018/IJHCITP.2016010101

Pessoa, C. R., & Júnior, M. D. (2017). A Telecommunications Approach in Systems for Effective Logistics and Supply Chains. In G. Jamil, A. Soares, & C. Pessoa (Eds.), *Handbook of Research on Information Management for Effective Logistics and Supply Chains* (pp. 437–452). Hershey, PA: IGI Global. doi:10.4018/978-1-5225-0973-8.ch023

Pessoa, C. R., & Marques, M. E. (2017). Information Technology and Communication Management in Supply Chain Management. In G. Jamil, A. Soares, & C. Pessoa (Eds.), *Handbook of Research on Information Management for Effective Logistics and Supply Chains* (pp. 23–33). Hershey, PA: IGI Global. doi:10.4018/978-1-5225-0973-8.ch002

Pinto-Llorente, A. M., Sánchez-Gómez, M. C., & García-Peñalvo, F. J. (2018). Students Skills in a Blended Learning Environment: A Qualitative Research. In A. Borchers (Ed.), *Technology Management in Organizational and Societal Contexts* (pp. 249–280). Hershey, PA: IGI Global. doi:10.4018/978-1-5225-5279-6.ch011

Poças Rascão, J. (2017). Information System for Logistics and Distribution Management. In G. Jamil, A. Soares, & C. Pessoa (Eds.), *Handbook of Research on Information Management for Effective Logistics and Supply Chains* (pp. 374–414). Hershey, PA: IGI Global. doi:10.4018/978-1-5225-0973-8.ch021

Pun, K. F., & Yiu, M. Y. (2018). Assessing Knowledge Management Performance in Organisations Based on the Criteria of Total Quality Management. In W. Lee & F. Sabetzadeh (Eds.), *Contemporary Knowledge and Systems Science* (pp. 224–255). Hershey, PA: IGI Global. doi:10.4018/978-1-5225-5655-8.ch009

Rafay, A., & Khan, A. (2018). Synergy for Sustainability in the Upcoming Telecommunications Revolution: The Case of a Developing Economy. In A. Borchers (Ed.), *Technology Management in Organizational and Societal Contexts* (pp. 51–76). Hershey, PA: IGI Global. doi:10.4018/978-1-5225-5279-6.ch003

Raghunath, K. M., Devi, S. L., & Patro, C. S. (2017). An Empirical Take on Qualitative and Quantitative Risk Factors. *International Journal of Risk and Contingency Management, 6*(4), 1–15. doi:10.4018/IJRCM.2017100101

Reed, A. H., & Angolia, M. (2018). Risk Management Usage and Impact on Information Systems Project Success. *International Journal of Information Technology Project Management, 9*(2), 1–19. doi:10.4018/IJITPM.2018040101

Reed, A. H., & Angolia, M. G. (2018). The Value of Simulation for Learning Project Management. In T. Bagwell, R. Cropf, & S. Foster-Gadkari (Eds.), *Information Technology as a Facilitator of Social Processes in Project Management and Collaborative Work* (pp. 21–39). Hershey, PA: IGI Global. doi:10.4018/978-1-5225-3471-6.ch002

Rincon, I. D. (2018). A Framework for Understanding the Role of Project Culture for Organizational Project Maturity. In G. Silvius & G. Karayaz (Eds.), *Developing Organizational Maturity for Effective Project Management* (pp. 154–168). Hershey, PA: IGI Global. doi:10.4018/978-1-5225-3197-5.ch008

Rodriguez, E., & Edwards, J. S. (2019). Knowledge Management in Support of Enterprise Risk Management. In M. Jennex (Ed.), *Effective Knowledge Management Systems in Modern Society* (pp. 284–307). Hershey, PA: IGI Global. doi:10.4018/978-1-5225-5427-1.ch014

Romano, L. (2017). Adaptive Portfolio Management. In L. Romano (Ed.), *Project Portfolio Management Strategies for Effective Organizational Operations* (pp. 153–177). Hershey, PA: IGI Global. doi:10.4018/978-1-5225-2151-8.ch006

Romano, L. (2017). Portfolio Management as a Step into the Future. In L. Romano (Ed.), *Project Portfolio Management Strategies for Effective Organizational Operations* (pp. 1–38). Hershey, PA: IGI Global. doi:10.4018/978-1-5225-2151-8.ch001

Romano, L., Grimaldi, R., & Colasuonno, F. S. (2017). Demand Management as a Success Factor in Project Portfolio Management. In L. Romano (Ed.), *Project Portfolio Management Strategies for Effective Organizational Operations* (pp. 202–219). Hershey, PA: IGI Global. doi:10.4018/978-1-5225-2151-8.ch008

Sarasa, A. (2018). An App to Manage Grammar Level Tests in Language Schools. In A. Borchers (Ed.), *Technology Management in Organizational and Societal Contexts* (pp. 169–197). Hershey, PA: IGI Global. doi:10.4018/978-1-5225-5279-6.ch008

Sargent, W. H., & Ferreira, G. A. (2018). Strategies to Improve Project Management Maturity. In G. Silvius & G. Karayaz (Eds.), *Developing Organizational Maturity for Effective Project Management* (pp. 279–295). Hershey, PA: IGI Global. doi:10.4018/978-1-5225-3197-5.ch014

Searight, B. K., & Spannaus, T. (2018). Online Learning: A Collaborative Perspective. In T. Bagwell, R. Cropf, & S. Foster-Gadkari (Eds.), *Information Technology as a Facilitator of Social Processes in Project Management and Collaborative Work* (pp. 83–98). Hershey, PA: IGI Global. doi:10.4018/978-1-5225-3471-6.ch005

Shehabat, I. M., & Berrish, M. (2018). Integration Between Knowledge Management and Total Quality Management in Jordanian Universities: Empirical Study. In W. Lee & F. Sabetzadeh (Eds.), *Contemporary Knowledge and Systems Science* (pp. 256–295). Hershey, PA: IGI Global. doi:10.4018/978-1-5225-5655-8.ch010

Silvius, G. (2018). Developing Project Management Maturity as an Organizational Change Process. In G. Silvius & G. Karayaz (Eds.), *Developing Organizational Maturity for Effective Project Management* (pp. 296–308). Hershey, PA: IGI Global. doi:10.4018/978-1-5225-3197-5.ch015

Simão, J. C., & Fernandes da Anunciação, P. (2017). Port Single Window and Logistics Single Window: Two Competitiveness Proposals in the Port Value Chain. In G. Jamil, A. Soares, & C. Pessoa (Eds.), *Handbook of Research on Information Management for Effective Logistics and Supply Chains* (pp. 316–333). Hershey, PA: IGI Global. doi:10.4018/978-1-5225-0973-8.ch018

Singh, N., Mittal, T., & Gupta, M. (2018). A Tale of Policies and Breaches: Analytical Approach to Construct Social Media Policy. In M. Gupta, R. Sharman, J. Walp, & P. Mulgund (Eds.), *Information Technology Risk Management and Compliance in Modern Organizations* (pp. 176–212). Hershey, PA: IGI Global. doi:10.4018/978-1-5225-2604-9.ch007

Skaik, H., & Othman, R. (2018). Exploring the Determinants Affecting Academics' Knowledge-Sharing Behavior in United Arab Emirates Public Universities. In W. Lee & F. Sabetzadeh (Eds.), *Contemporary Knowledge and Systems Science* (pp. 151–191). Hershey, PA: IGI Global. doi:10.4018/978-1-5225-5655-8.ch007

Soares, E. R., & Zaidan, F. H. (2017). Composition of the Financial Logistic Costs of the IT Organizations Linked to the Financial Market: Financial Indicators of the Software Development Project. In G. Jamil, A. Soares, & C. Pessoa (Eds.), *Handbook of Research on Information Management for Effective Logistics and Supply Chains* (pp. 255–272). Hershey, PA: IGI Global. doi:10.4018/978-1-5225-0973-8.ch014

Soni, P. (2018). Implications of HIPAA and Subsequent Regulations on Information Technology. In M. Gupta, R. Sharman, J. Walp, & P. Mulgund (Eds.), *Information Technology Risk Management and Compliance in Modern Organizations* (pp. 71–98). Hershey, PA: IGI Global. doi:10.4018/978-1-5225-2604-9.ch004

Sousa, M. J., Cruz, R., Dias, I., & Caracol, C. (2017). Information Management Systems in the Supply Chain. In G. Jamil, A. Soares, & C. Pessoa (Eds.), *Handbook of Research on Information Management for Effective Logistics and Supply Chains* (pp. 469–485). Hershey, PA: IGI Global. doi:10.4018/978-1-5225-0973-8.ch025

Styhre, A. (2018). Theorizing Sociomaterial Practices: Gilbert Simondon's Theory of Individuation. In W. Lee & F. Sabetzadeh (Eds.), *Contemporary Knowledge and Systems Science* (pp. 38–49). Hershey, PA: IGI Global. doi:10.4018/978-1-5225-5655-8.ch002

Suresh, N., & Gupta, M. (2018). Impact of Technology Innovation: A Study on Cloud Risk Mitigation. In M. Gupta, R. Sharman, J. Walp, & P. Mulgund (Eds.), *Information Technology Risk Management and Compliance in Modern Organizations* (pp. 229–267). Hershey, PA: IGI Global. doi:10.4018/978-1-5225-2604-9.ch009

Tichenor, C. (2018). The Mythical Lines of Code Metric: A Form of Moral Hazard. In T. Bagwell, R. Cropf, & S. Foster-Gadkari (Eds.), *Information Technology as a Facilitator of Social Processes in Project Management and Collaborative Work* (pp. 124–143). Hershey, PA: IGI Global. doi:10.4018/978-1-5225-3471-6.ch007

Yazici, H. J. (2018). Role of Organizational Project Maturity on Business Success: Last Five Years' Outlook and Beyond. In G. Silvius & G. Karayaz (Eds.), *Developing Organizational Maturity for Effective Project Management* (pp. 43–54). Hershey, PA: IGI Global. doi:10.4018/978-1-5225-3197-5.ch003

Yeşil, S., & Hırlak, B. (2019). Exploring Knowledge-Sharing Barriers and Their Implications. In M. Jennex (Ed.), *Effective Knowledge Management Systems in Modern Society* (pp. 99–122). Hershey, PA: IGI Global. doi:10.4018/978-1-5225-5427-1.ch006

Zhou, C. (2018). Supporting Creative Learning by Information Communication Technology (ICT) in Project Teams. In T. Bagwell, R. Cropf, & S. Foster-Gadkari (Eds.), *Information Technology as a Facilitator of Social Processes in Project Management and Collaborative Work* (pp. 1–20). Hershey, PA: IGI Global. doi:10.4018/978-1-5225-3471-6.ch001

Zuchi, D. (2018). The Maturity of the Project Owner: How Can It Be Developed? In G. Silvius & G. Karayaz (Eds.), *Developing Organizational Maturity for Effective Project Management* (pp. 201–209). Hershey, PA: IGI Global. doi:10.4018/978-1-5225-3197-5.ch010

Index

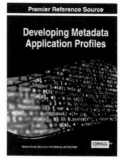

Ensure Quality Research is Introduced to the Academic Community

Become an IGI Global Reviewer for Authored Book Projects

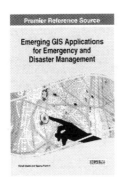

Premier Reference Source

Emerging GIS Applications for Emergency and Disaster Management

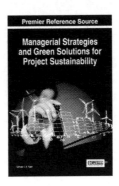

Premier Reference Source

Managerial Strategies and Green Solutions for Project Sustainability

Premier Reference Source

Comparative Approaches to Using R and Python for Statistical Data Analysis

Premier Reference Source

Solutions for High-Touch Communications in a High-Tech World

The overall success of an authored book project is dependent on quality and timely reviews.

In this competitive age of scholarly publishing, constructive and timely feedback significantly expedites the turnaround time of manuscripts from submission to acceptance, allowing the publication and discovery of forward-thinking research at a much more expeditious rate. Several IGI Global authored book projects are currently seeking highly qualified experts in the field to fill vacancies on their respective editorial review boards:

Applications may be sent to:
development@igi-global.com

Applicants must have a doctorate (or an equivalent degree) as well as publishing and reviewing experience. Reviewers are asked to write reviews in a timely, collegial, and constructive manner. All reviewers will begin their role on an ad-hoc basis for a period of one year, and upon successful completion of this term can be considered for full editorial review board status, with the potential for a subsequent promotion to Associate Editor.

If you have a colleague that may be interested in this opportunity, we encourage you to share this information with them.

The Premier Reference for Information Science & Information Technology

100% Original Content
Contains 705 new, peer-reviewed articles with color figures covering over 80 categories in 11 subject areas

Diverse Contributions
More than 1,100 experts from 74 unique countries contributed their specialized knowledge

Easy Navigation
Includes two tables of content and a comprehensive index in each volume for the user's convenience

Highly-Cited
Embraces a complete list of references and additional reading sections to allow for further research

Included in:
InfoSci®-Books

Encyclopedia of Information Science and Technology Fourth Edition
A Comprehensive 10-Volume Set

Mehdi Khosrow-Pour, D.B.A. (Information Resources Management Association, USA)
ISBN: 978-1-5225-2255-3; © 2018; Pg: 8,104; Release Date: July 2017

For a limited time, _receive the complimentary e-books for the First, Second, and Third editions_ with the purchase of the _Encyclopedia of Information Science and Technology, Fourth Edition_ e-book.*

The **Encyclopedia of Information Science and Technology, Fourth Edition** is a 10-volume set which includes 705 original and previously unpublished research articles covering a full range of perspectives, applications, and techniques contributed by thousands of experts and researchers from around the globe. This authoritative encyclopedia is an all-encompassing, well-established reference source that is ideally designed to disseminate the most forward-thinking and diverse research findings. With critical perspectives on the impact of information science management and new technologies in modern settings, including but not limited to computer science, education, healthcare, government, engineering, business, and natural and physical sciences, it is a pivotal and relevant source of knowledge that will benefit every professional within the field of information science and technology and is an invaluable addition to every academic and corporate library.

Scan for Online Bookstore

Pricing Information

Hardcover: **$5,695**   E-Book: **$5,695**   Hardcover + E-Book: **$6,895**

Both E-Book Prices Include:
- Encyclopedia of Information Science and Technology, First Edition E-Book
- Encyclopedia of Information Science and Technology, Second Edition E-Book
- Encyclopedia of Information Science and Technology, Third Edition E-Book

*Purchase the Encyclopedia of Information Science and Technology, Fourth Edition e-book and receive the first, second, and third e-book editions for free. Offer is only valid with purchase of the fourth edition's e-book through the IGI Global Online Bookstore.

Recommend this Title to Your Institution's Library: www.igi-global.com/books

Printed in the United States
By Bookmasters